Some books teach us truth, others motivate us, and some show us how to apply what we know. Rarely does a book do all three, but *Discipology* does. You'll understand disciple-making at a new level by reading this important book.

Ed Stetzer, dean, Talbot School of Theology

Peyton's best book yet. Starting with a groundbreaking premise, this christological work offers a practical framework for moving from talking about discipleship to actual disciple-making.

Brian Sanders, founder and executive director, Underground Network

Peyton Jones beautifully weds orthodoxy with orthopraxy. He applies first-century principles to a twenty-first-century context with clarity and conviction. This book will reorient your ministry around Jesus's rhythms and cultivate real disciple-making movement.

Dhati Lewis, president, MyBLVD; visionary pastor, Blueprint Church

If you want to do discipleship the Jesus way and see spectators become "sent ones," *Discipology* is the clearest and most compelling road map I've seen. A must-read for every leader.

Dr. Larry Walkemeyer, global pastor, Light & Life Church

Discipology is field-tested, grounded in Scripture, and refreshingly practical.

Dave Ferguson, CEO, Exponential

Peyton reframes disciple-making as the missing engine of genuine movement: mobilization before multiplication. This field-tested guide calls leaders to move from managing churches to activating people into Jesus's mission.

Brad Brisco, author, *Missional Essentials*

In *Discipology*, Peyton Jones unpacks scriptural principles in ways you can't unsee. The discipleship patterns he uncovers from Jesus and Paul are theologically rich and practical. I'll revisit these principles again and again.

Karl Vaters, contributor at Helping Small Churches Thrive

Peyton Jones brings us back to the compelling genius of Jesus's disciple-making strategy—biblical, practical, and urgently needed for leaders shaping a culture of multiplication today.

Dr. Ed Love, executive director of church multiplication and discipleship, The Wesleyan Church

Jesus gave the church one commission: to make disciples. Too many Christians don't know what this means. *Discipology* challenges and encourages us to rediscover the lost art of disciple-making for the twenty-first century.

Dr. Winfield Bevins, founder, Creo Arts; author, *How Beauty Will Save the World*

This brilliant, accessible work dives into the source code of discipleship: the person and ministry of Jesus. Jones lays out a simple, reproducible process that revolutionized Palestine and sets the foundation for us to follow.

Mike Chong Perkinson, PCJC Network Lead

Finally, a practical, theologically grounded field guide for disciple-making. Peyton breaks down Jesus's methods so everyone can get off the pew and on mission.

Rev. Dr. Deb Walkemeyer, strategic catalyst for multiplication, Free Methodist Church USA

Over decades, the church has morphed discipleship into programs. Peyton dismantles myths and restores Jesus's timeless, joyful model of discipleship. *Discipology* revitalizes and excites believers to reengage in disciple-making.

Andy Froiland, pastor

Warning: If you're content with your current view of discipleship, don't read this book! Peyton Jones disruptively reveals the revolutionary nature of the early church and shows how to step into Jesus's rhythms of disciple-making.

Steve Pike, founder, Next Wave Community

Jesus's parting words matter: "Go and make disciples!" Most of us have grown up in a church-growth world, so making churches seemed like a good idea. But what about the 60 to 70 percent of people who will never enter a church? Read this book. Then go!

Greg Wigfield, lead pastor, Destiny Church

In church planting, we often get the cart before the horse: Plant a church, then make disciples. *Discipology* reminds us that everything in ministry starts with making disciples.

Frank Wooden, executive director, Plant SoCal

Discipology bridges the gap between learning about discipleship and making disciples in everyday life. Peyton offers clear, engaging insights that reflect how Jesus trained his disciples.

Cathy Tastad, superintendent, The Pacific Northwest Conference of the Free Methodist Church

Most discipleship ends with the last page of a book or sermon. In *Discipology*, Peyton Jones reveals what's been hiding in plain sight: Mobilization precedes movement. He provides a clear, Jesus-inspired pathway to mobilize believers into disciple-makers.

David Sunde, pastor; author, *Homegrown Disciples*

Jones is both prophetic and pragmatic, inspiring and instructional. *Discipology* is a clarion call back to Jesus's original blueprint for making and mobilizing disciples, equipping the church to reimagine its future.

Rich Robinson, founder and director, 5Q Collective

In a world where discipleship programs abound but impact little, Peyton Jones offers a practical methodology that mobilizes. *Discipology* combines Jesus's practices with generations of wisdom in a framework that feels both time-tested and fresh.

Jessie Cruickshank, author, *Ordinary Discipleship*

JOURNEY TO DISCIPLE-MAKING

PEYTON JONES

JOURNEY TO DISCIPLE-MAKING

A Discipology Journal

ZONDERVAN REFLECTIVE

EX EXPONENTIAL RESOURCES

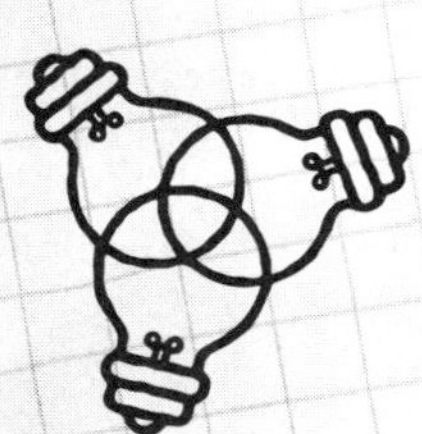

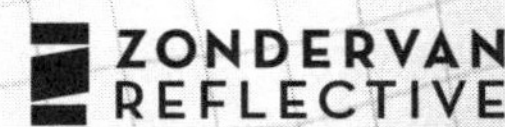

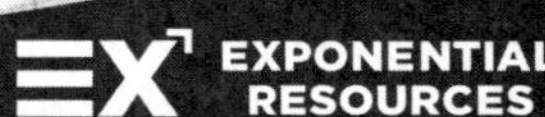

ZONDERVAN REFLECTIVE

Journey to Disciple-Making

Published by Zondervan, 3950 Sparks Drive SE, Suite 101, Grand Rapids, MI 49546, USA. Zondervan is a registered trademark of The Zondervan Corporation, L.L.C., a wholly owned subsidiary of HarperCollins Christian Publishing, Inc.

Requests for information should be addressed to customercare@harpercollins.com.

Zondervan titles may be purchased in bulk for educational, business, fundraising, or sales promotional use. For information, please email SpecialMarkets@Zondervan.com.

ISBN 978-0-310-18036-4 (softcover)
ISBN 978-0-310-18037-1 (ebook)

Author represented by The Steve Laube Agency.

HarperCollins Publishers, Macken House, 39/40 Mayor Street Upper, Dublin 1, D01 C9W8, Ireland (https://www.harpercollins.com)

Cover design: Jonlin Creative
Cover art: © ArtBalitskiy, Primiaou, Mariia Levchenko, Viktoriia Ablohina, Ulimi / Getty Images
Interior design: Denise Froehlich
Interior images: © stock.adobe.com

Printed in the United States of America

26 27 28 29 30 31 32 33 / TRM / 10 9 8 7 6 5 4 3 2 1

Contents

RHYTHM 3: TACTICS: SENDING DISCIPLES

A JOURNEY THROUGH JOHN

Welcome to the Journey

So . . . you've never made a disciple before?

Perfect. You're in exactly the right place. Welcome to *Journey to Disciple-Making: A Discipology Journal*. If you're holding this journal wondering if it's really for *you*—if maybe there's been some sort of divine delivery error and this was meant for someone holier, smarter, more qualified—let me stop you right there.

This *is* for you.

You don't have to be a pastor, a Bible scholar, or some kind of spiritual superhero to make disciples. You only have to be willing to follow Jesus and help someone else do the same.

You might be thinking, *Wait, that's it? I thought "go make disciples" meant "go start painfully awkward conversations with complete strangers" or "go to the ends of the earth to convert the masses."*

Nope. Follow Jesus. Help someone else follow Jesus. That's it.

If that sounds simple . . . well, it is. But it's also messy, stretching, transformative, and above all, exhilarating. It's also the most eternally meaningful thing you'll ever do with your life.

And the best part? You won't be alone. Jesus will be right there *with you*.

But you'll also have an additional friend with you. Jesus sent out the disciples in twos, and it worked! We're going to use a lot of the same strategies that Jesus used. After all, he's the one who called us to make disciples, so it makes sense to do it his way. Plus, it's nice to have someone with you when you're trying something new. And there will be some experimentation along the way.

If you're new to making disciples, you're probably scratching your head about the *how* of it all. It's normal to not know where to start. Fortunately, Jesus modeled disciple-making for three years. What follows in this book is not my blueprint for disciple-making but Jesus's. When I started this adventure, my aim was not to invent a clever new system but to rediscover the strategy that was already there—the same one Jesus used to transform twelve misfit knuckleheads from the Gospels into the active disciples in Acts.

Even though Jesus created this great system, you might not think you can pull it off. But it is more within your reach than you realize—you just need to know the tactics. Journalist Joshua Foer heard the reigning memory champion claim that anyone with an average memory could become the next memory champion if they learned the right techniques. Foer laughed it off, thinking memory champions were born with photographic minds. The memory champion pressed harder, "No, if you follow these techniques, you can do it too." One year later, employing those techniques, Foer, who previously couldn't remember where he left his car keys, was crowned the USA Memory Champion.[1] Foer became the memory champ by learning the *how*—and the *how* of disciple-making is what this journal is all about, meaning you can do it too.

Think of this book as a guide for your journey of discovery—both a lab manual and a notebook to record your own transformation as you experiment with making disciples. Rather than a book to read once and shelve, it's a fifty-two-step process of transformation. And transformation means change.

We've all tried the "read some verses, feel warm fuzzies, go back to life as usual" kind of change. But deep down, we all long for the "Wow, I'm not the same person I was when I started" kind of change. Enough of that and you have *change the world* kind of change.

If you've never made a disciple before but are willing to take those shaky first steps with Jesus—to walk alongside him—to discover how *he* made disciples, and then try it out right where you are in your everyday life, this journal is for you. Each step gives a bite-size chunk of how Jesus made disciples, followed by a chance to reflect on the principles with others, and finally one simple action step.

And here's how it works: With each step, you'll start by reading a short devotional in this journal, reflect personally on the principles, and then commit to taking one simple action step. But you won't be walking through it with just paper and ink—you'll also have the help of Through the Word's ten-minute audio guides. Each step in the journal is paired with an audio teaching that unpacks Scripture in the same way the disciples once heard Jesus unpack it on the road. Think of it as your companion voice, connecting the dots and walking alongside you through the text. That's where you'll also have the opportunity to compare notes and discuss with your disciple-making partner within a shared group on the Through the Word—Discipology Plan.

---

1. Joshua Foer, *Moonwalking with Einstein: The Art and Science of Remembering Everything* (New York: Penguin Press, 2011), 6–7.

Journal in hand, earphones in, steps on the ground—that's how the learning sinks in and the transformation takes root. Over time those steps add up to a whole new way of walking—following Jesus more closely and helping others do the same.

Summary:

1. Read the devotional.
2. Journal your personal reflections.
3. Commit to the action step.
4. Listen to the ten-minute audio guide in your Discipology Plan on Through the Word.
5. Interact with your disciple-making partner within the app.

(If you're the kind of person who really appreciates a pocket protector and a slide rule for a deeper dive, then see the appendix: "How to Use This Book" on page 217.)

The transformations of Jesus's closest followers were captured in the pages of the Gospels. Within its pages, we get a front-row seat to Jesus transforming confused nobodies into courageous world-changers. But what about *your* story? This journal is your snapshot in time—something you can return to years from now to remember how fresh and sweet this journey was when it was all just beginning. Because coming behind you are people who never saw themselves making disciples—just like you—and they'll need to hear *your* story. Because if you're willing to go on this journey with Jesus, you'll never be the same again.

INTRODUCTION TO DISCIPLE-MAKING

Thomas Edison didn't invent the lightbulb.

That actually surprises a lot of people. You see, the dream of electric light wasn't new. Other inventors had gotten close, and before Edison came along there were over twenty different versions of clunky prototypes that burned out too fast or were too dim to be useful.

The world was dark after sunset, lit only by candles, gas lamps, and flickering lanterns. The pieces were there—filaments, glass, current—but nothing *worked*. Not for long, anyway. The light always fizzled, burned out, or couldn't handle the current. Edison and his team tested over six thousand materials for filaments yet failed repeatedly. Then one day his team discovered a carbonized bamboo filament. They flipped the switch . . . and *the light stayed on*!

What came next was more than just a brighter room. It was a brighter *world*. And here's the thing: **The power had always been there.**

Edison didn't invent electricity. He just provided a way to conduct it. He had discovered the means of harnessing one spark that could light up thousands. Disciple-making is supposed to work like that: One person's life carrying the light of Jesus to another until whole communities begin to glow. It's not about flashy brilliance but sustainable and transferable power. A simple, Spirit-empowered process that changes everything.

Disciple-making is about connecting other lightbulbs to the source: Jesus.

Edison is reported to have famously said, "I have not failed. I've just found ten thousand ways that won't work."[1] I love that God doesn't require us to have it all figured out or be perfect

1. Thomas Edison, *Oxford Essential Quotations*, ed. Susan Ratcliffe (Oxford University Press, 2016).

at disciple-making. He gave us the principles, if we'll pay attention to what Jesus did, but allows us to experiment and have fun. In case you're wondering—you can't screw this up. You just gotta screw in yourself to the One who has the power. And as you shine his light, others will be drawn to it and want to follow him too.

John, who walked with Jesus for more years than anyone, put it like this, "Walk in the light, as he is in the light" (1 John 1:7).

On the journey of disciple-making, we are walking in the light. Jesus made two increasingly profound statements about light: "I am the light of the world" (John 8:12) and "You are the light of the world" (Matt. 5:14). That means he expects us to shine his light for others now through making disciples. If you've ever attempted to walk a path in the darkness, you know that navigating without light feels impossible. That's why you and your "two" will be coming alongside a "who" like someone with a flashlight. Your own light will help them see Jesus as you walk alongside them, guiding them until they're able to plug into him themselves.

Walking in the light and bringing someone alongside you on the journey is what disciple-making is all about.

DATE ____ / ____ / ____

STEP 1

Who Makes Disciples?

When Simon Peter saw this, he fell at Jesus' knees and said, "Go away from me, Lord; I am a sinful man!"

—LUKE 5:8

You were always the wrong guy. Until you weren't.

—LAURA, DEADPOOL & WOLVERINE

Today's Teaching

I know what you're thinking: *Me? A disciple-maker? You've got the wrong person.*

Peter thought that too. Imagine with me what it must have been like to be Peter two thousand years ago . . .

Jesus turned to Peter in the boat with that familiar tone that sounded like a suggestion but landed like a command: "Put out into the deep water and let down your nets for a catch."

Peter blinked, caught off guard. "Rabbi," he said, sighing, "we were out all night. Not a single fish . . ." Then he added with a reluctant smile, "But because it's you, I'll do it."

The net hit the water with a familiar slap, sinking into the deep like it had a thousand times before. Peter gave it a token tug, half expecting it to drag in the same silent disappointment. But then it jolted. Hard. Like the sea itself had clenched its fist. The rope tightened, screamed against his calloused palms. Peter shouted, and the others leaped to help as the boat lurched sideways under the weight. Fish—too many to count—thrashed and shimmered like silver fire beneath the surface. The net strained, on the brink of bursting. Another boat was signaled, and they came fast, both vessels groaning with the load, sinking under the sheer glory of it. And right there—knee-deep in fish and salt water—Peter fell to his knees, eyes wide, breath stolen and said not "Thank you," but "Go away from me, Lord; I am a sinful man!"

Wow . . . why did Peter react with shame instead of excitement?

Because sometimes when grace floods the boat, the first thing you feel isn't worthy—it's undone. Peter thinks Jesus has the wrong person, but the right people always feel that way.

Then came the words that changed everything. Jesus didn't say, "Follow me and try harder." Or "from now on you'll have to do better—be better, Peter." He didn't say, "Follow me and prove yourself." He said, "Follow me, and I will make you . . ." The call wasn't to earn something but to be made into something—*something they weren't yet*. They were fishermen, yes. But not fishers of other people.

"Follow me, and I will make you fishers of people."

It was a call to make disciples. Peter understood that Jesus was inviting him to do for others what was done for him: extend an invitation of grace, inviting others to follow Jesus. And he couldn't help but feel unworthy. Perhaps Jesus picked Peter because he felt like the least qualified person on earth to make disciples. So that he could encourage others who also saw themselves as unlikely candidates, the kind who might be deemed "Least Likely to Be Used By God" in their high school yearbook.

If you see your own picture under that title, you're in good company—with the people

God uses most. Peter had a knack for screwing up spectacularly—he blew it with style. After denying Jesus three times, he could hardly forgive himself. But Jesus did. He also used Peter fifty-one days later to lead more than three thousand people to Jesus in a single day. That's how God uses people. He takes the people most desperate for grace and turns them into the biggest billboards for it.

Hmmm . . . fifty-one days . . . about the same length as this journal if you're doing it daily. I wonder what God could do with you in that span of time.

Consider this cast of unlikely characters God used to do great things, despite them excusing themselves as lost causes:

Moses said he couldn't speak well (Ex. 4:10–13).
Jeremiah said he was too young (Jer. 1:6).
Gideon said he was the weakest (Judg. 6:14–15).
Saul (the first king of Israel) said he was from the smallest tribe (1 Sam. 9:21).
Isaiah said he had a dirty mouth (Isa. 6:5).
Jonah didn't want to go at all (Jonah 1:1–3).
Sarah laughed and thought, I'm too old (Gen. 18:12–15).
Abraham thought God's plan sounded ridiculous (Gen. 17:17).
Elijah would rather have died than do what God asked him (1 Kings 19:4).
Zechariah (John the Baptist's father) doubted what the angel told him (Luke 1:18–20).
Timothy struggled with insecurity (1 Tim. 4:12).
Paul thought he was the chief of sinners and struggled with his past (1 Cor. 15:9).

God used these people in many ways, despite their insecurities and flaws. But some, including Paul saw God use his unworthiness: "I received mercy for this reason, that in me, as the foremost, Jesus Christ might display his perfect patience as an example to those who were to believe in him for eternal life" (1 Tim. 1:16 ESV). A billboard of grace, shining like a lightbulb.

We weren't made to shine out who we are but to illuminate who *he* is so others can see him.

Yet even with your light shining, it's easy to feel unqualified or inadequate. Like Peter, we all have our reasons why God shouldn't use us. But God has never let those reasons stop him using people before, so why should he start with you?

When God calls us to make disciples, he *takes* us as we are but doesn't *leave* us where we are. Jesus told the disciples that if they followed him, he would *make* them fishers of people. That was a promise to make them something they were not. And to make you something you are not . . . yet.

In Ephesians 2:10, Paul writes, "We are God's handiwork, created in Christ Jesus to do good works, which God prepared in advance for us to do." Paul is saying you are handcrafted by God for works he already planned for you in advance. Just as he had a path for Peter, for Paul, for John, he's got one for you. That means he's got people out there waiting to be discipled by you. And if you're his handiwork, there's nobody else like you—snowflake status confirmed. You were designed for disciple-making. Despite any doubts you may feel, Paul is saying you were quite literally *made for this*.

On this journey, Jesus will show you how. So to answer the question, *Who makes disciples?* People just like you.

Pray This

Jesus, I know I'm not a special case. You've shown who you are through people just like me for thousands of years. I confess I often feel unqualified to make disciples, but then I remember that it's something you asked me to do. Please make me transparent in more ways than one. First, help me to be honest about my faults and inadequacies. But also help me to be so transparent that people see you, *not me.*

Today's Time

* When you hear the phrase *disciple-maker*, what feelings come to mind? Why do you think that is?
* Do you see your life as a lightbulb shining on Jesus? Or are you concerned people can't look past your flaws, faults, and frailty?
* What's one hope or dream you have for what God could do through you?

Today's Tactic: Finding Your Two

If you haven't already, it's time to grab your "two" and get them started on this journey with you. Think of them as your lab partner in your experiment of making disciples. You don't have to do this alone—Jesus sent his disciples out in pairs. Who might make an awesome walking partner on this disciple-making journey? Don't worry if they feel as inadequate as you do. You can immediately share with them what you've learned today.

- Write your name in the lightbulb on the left. Then write their name in the lightbulb on the right.

- Scan the QR code to start your journey on the Discipology Plan in the Through the Word app. Remember, this is your "on the go" training where you can interact with your disciple-making partner (or your "two"). You can invite your "two" directly from inside the app.
- Invite your two, and listen to today's audio on the Discipology Plan. It'll take ten minutes.

Big Idea: God delights in using unlikely people. If you feel unqualified, you're in good company.

Your Lightbulb Moment —

DATE ___ / ___ / ___

STEP 2

What Is Disciple-Making?

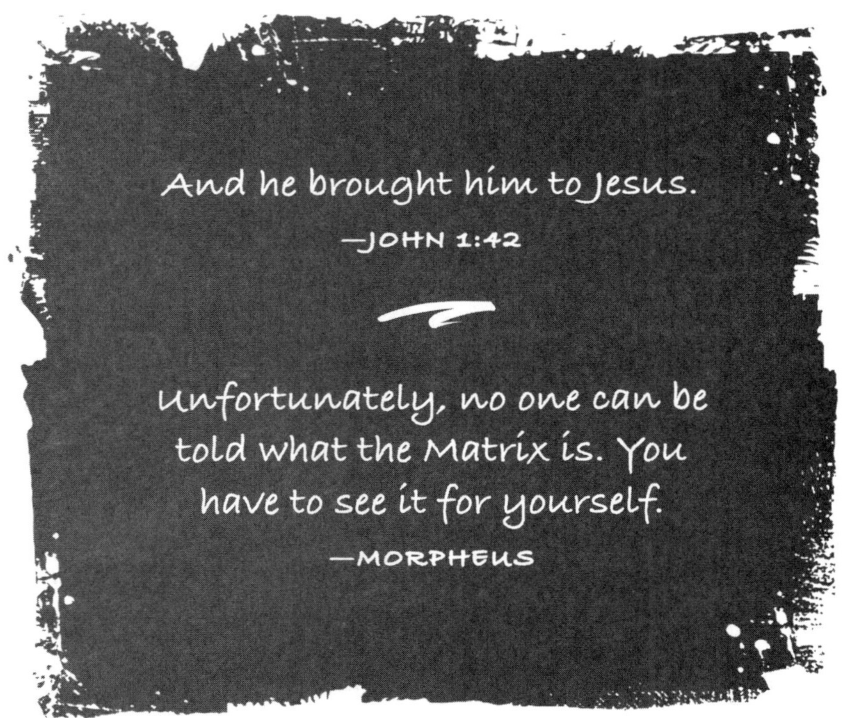

Today's Teaching

Welcome back. First steps are often about curiosity, but second steps are about moving forward. So, well done on showing up for the second step! Every additional step you take on this journey builds momentum on the walk toward disciple-making.

In the last step, we talked about Jesus calling Peter to make disciples. What many people don't know is that Peter already knew Jesus for a year before being invited to become a "fisher of people" and leaving his nets to follow Jesus full-time. Peter's story gives us one of the clearest pictures of disciple-making and how simple it really is.

It started with his brother Andrew, who'd only just had dinner with Jesus. John 1:41–42 tells us, "The first thing Andrew did was to find his brother Simon and tell him, 'We have found the Messiah' (that is, the Christ). And he brought him to Jesus."

That's what disciple-making is:

Following Jesus and bringing others with you.

Peter follows Andrew to meet Jesus. John records the moment like this: "And he brought him to Jesus. Jesus looked at him and said, 'You are Simon son of John. You will be called Cephas' (which, when translated, is Peter)" (John 1:42).

The phrase "Jesus looked at him" means more than a glance; it means a studying gaze. After a pause, Jesus spoke: "You are Simon son of John." That alone likely startled Simon. How could this stranger know his name, let alone his father's? But then came something stranger still: "You will be called [Peter]."

Jesus gave Simon a new nickname that day, one he'd need to grow into. The name Peter means "rock"—in this case a foundation stone set in line with a cornerstone, something others could anchor to. But Simon was anything *but* stable—impulsive, volatile, quick to speak, and quick to stumble. Everyone knew Simon that way. But Jesus called him Peter, or "the rock," not for who he was but for who he would become.

That's an important part of disciple-making: seeing in the person you're discipling the potential of transformation once they plug into Jesus. Jesus saw the loyalty flickering inside Simon—the only one who would later step out of a boat in wavering faith and attempt to walk on water to get to Jesus. He'd also see Peter blunder zealously into mistakes, like grabbing a sword to defend Jesus and cutting someone's ear off.

For this reason, Jesus often called him by both names—"Simon" when correcting him, "Peter" when calling out his potential. Two names: one for the man he was, and one for the man he was becoming. Plugged into the light of Jesus, Peter's lamp burned bright at times and flickered dimly at others. So do ours. One moment we shine, the next we sputter. That's the disciple's journey—a mass of contradictions. Aren't we all? And as we disciple others, we need the same patience Jesus showed Peter—the same patience he shows *us*.

Just as Peter saw a light in Andrew that sparked his curiosity, people will also follow our imperfect light to get to Jesus. Listen to how John the Baptist was described: "He came as a witness to testify concerning that light, so that through him all might believe. *He himself was not the light;* he came only as a witness to the light. The true light that gives light to everyone was coming into the world" (John 1:7–9, emphasis mine).

Our light points to Jesus, the Light of the World. People will see our light shine—sometimes brightly, sometimes dimly—and somehow they'll still recognize their need for Jesus, the perfect and constant source of that light. Andrew had plugged into that light and lit the way for Peter, until Peter plugged into Jesus himself.

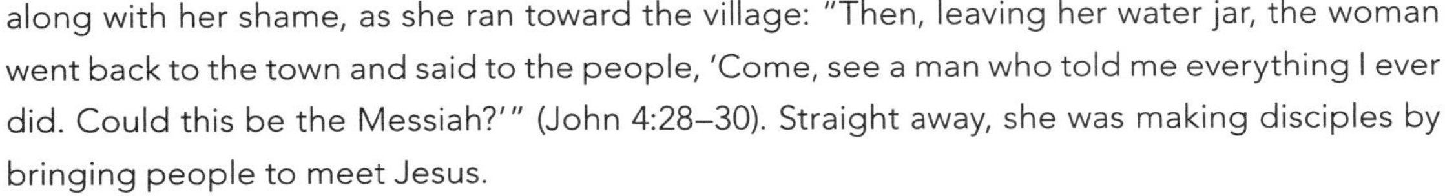

That's the essence of disciple-making—lighting the way to Jesus for others as you walk in his perfect light. The goal? To have them plug into Jesus directly so that they can experience his transformational power themselves.

The Samaritan woman at the well also brought others to Jesus. After one conversation with Jesus, she ditched her water jar in the dust, along with her shame, as she ran toward the village: "Then, leaving her water jar, the woman went back to the town and said to the people, 'Come, see a man who told me everything I ever did. Could this be the Messiah?'" (John 4:28–30). Straight away, she was making disciples by bringing people to meet Jesus.

The day after I started following Jesus, I called my best friend on the phone, Erik, and clumsily spoke into the receiver: "Hey man, I didn't know this, but yesterday, I was going to hell, just like you are now. I just talked to a guy and Jesus is real. He forgave me of everything I've done, and it feels incredible. You want to follow him with me?"

There was a slight pause on the other end.

"Okay."

We prayed—I have no idea what—but after my lame attempt to introduce Erik to Jesus, he is still walking with him nearly four decades later.

This is how disciple-making worked with Jesus's first few disciples in John 1:

1. Andrew and John met Jesus first.
2. Then Andrew fetched Peter.
3. John grabbed James.
4. Finally, Jesus called Philip with those familiar words, "Follow me," and Philip ran to get Nathanael.

It was that simple: "Follow me" and bring someone else.

Wanna know a shocker? Of the first six disciples, Jesus only called three of them directly: John, Andrew, and Philip.

John brought James.

Andrew brought Peter.

Philip brought Nathanael.

You and I can do that, right? Bring people to Jesus?

Disciple-making is that simple—just following Jesus and bringing others along with you, in hopes that they will follow him too. And you don't even have to know that much about him; knowing him is enough to get started.

Pray This

Jesus, thank you for finding me. I know I didn't stumble into your grace by accident; you reached me through the faithfulness of others. Someone prayed for me, someone spoke to me, someone showed me what you're like. I'm grateful to be part of that long chain of stories where you keep showing up. Now I ask that you make me a link in the chain for someone else. Use my words, my life, and my presence to point them toward you. I don't need to have all the answers; just help me to be faithful to share the part of the story you've written in me. Please do the same for my disciple-making partner today. May we both be faithful links in your work so that one day someone else will look back and thank you for reaching them through us.

Today's Time

- Whom did God use to reach you? How do you think they felt about God using them?
- Is it hard for you to tell someone why you follow Jesus?
- How does it feel to know that your imperfect light can still show someone the way to Jesus?

Today's Tactic: Identifying Potential Whos

Think about all your relationships today—people who already know you. For the woman it was her village. For John and Andrew, it was their brothers. For Philip, it was a friend.

Take five minutes to jot down **names of people you regularly connect with**: family, friends, coworkers, neighbors, teammates, classmates, or even casual acquaintances. People who haven't started walking with Jesus yet. This is how we begin to find your "who."

- Write your name in the center of this lightbulb.
- Around it, write the names of people you see intermittently throughout the year.
- Circle any who might be open to deeper friendship, faith conversations, or spiritual encouragement.
- Talk over all these names with your "two" today and how God could really transform their lives.

Big Idea: Disciple-making is simple: follow Jesus, and bring someone with you.

Your Lightbulb Moment —

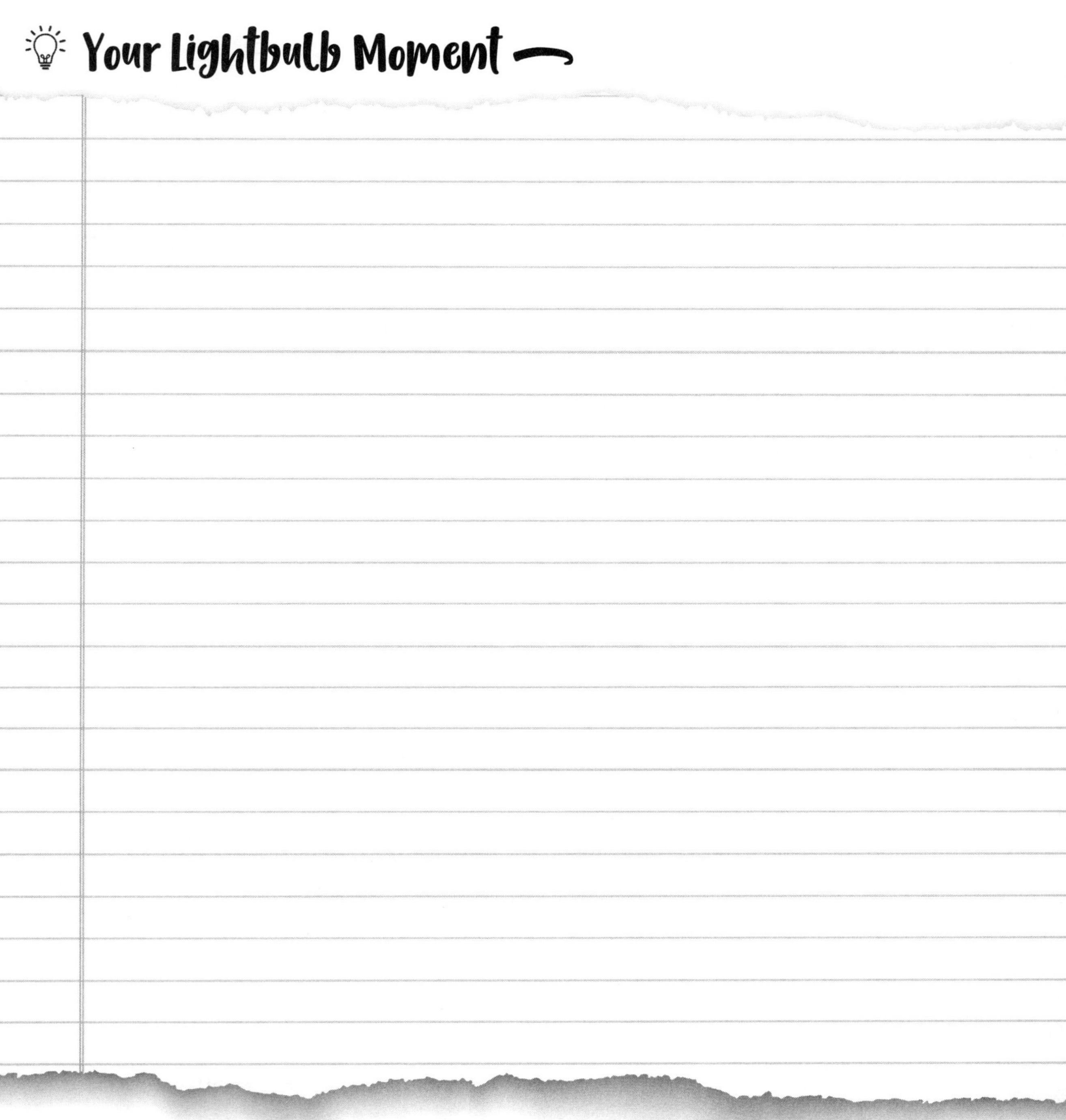

STEP 3

How Are Disciples Made?

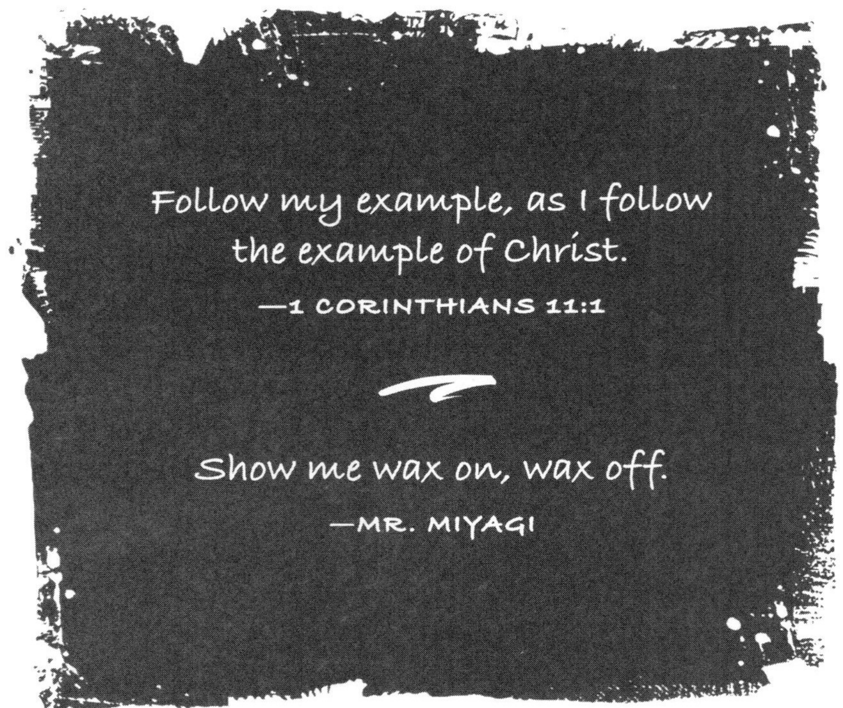

Today's Teaching

Welcome back. So far we've covered some serious ground on the first two steps of our journey:

Who makes disciples: You!

What disciple-making is: Following Jesus and bringing someone with you.

We know the *why*: Jesus said to . . . duh.

And today we'll talk about *how*. This is the big one that usually stops us.

Maybe you've sat in church listening to sermons about disciple-making and feel as pumped as someone who just watched a *Creed* film. In the 1970s people exited the *Rocky* showings and punched people in the head. Like them, you exit the church super inspired to swing out and step into the ring of disciple-making—except you don't know how to box. So we can know the what and why, but without the how we're pretty lost. But I have a theory:

We tend to make disciples in the same way we were discipled.

And if that's true, the flip side is also true: We tend to *not* make disciples just like we were *not* discipled.

If you weren't discipled yourself, it's not your fault if you don't know how to make disciples.

Most of us aren't being *disobedient*; we're just *disoriented*. According to a Barna research study, the majority of Christians polled say they'd love to make disciples but want "someone to teach them how to do it well."[1]

For many of us, our journey to becoming a disciple began something like this at the time of our conversion:

> You're saved! Welcome to the family of God—your whole life is about to change! Here's a Bible—1,000 pages, black leather, gold letters, no instructions. Next, pray. Don't worry if you don't know how; it's easy! Just talk to God like a friend. Oh, and tell others about Jesus too—they need it. Church is important—come back to get "fed." (Though you don't remember seeing any food.) Almost forgot—there's a devil. He hates you, wants to ruin your life. Watch out! Okay, bye!

1. Barna Group, *Growing Together* (Ventura, CA: Barna Group Publishing, 2020), 59.

It feels like jumping out of—no, scratch that—like being kicked out of an airplane for the first time with no preparation. Someone thrusts a parachute pack into your arms, smiles, and says, "Good luck out there, but don't forget to pull the rip cord!" as their foot lands squarely in your gut. And as you plummet to earth, you wonder what a rip cord even is . . . and how to use it.

But let me assure you that if you weren't discipled or have no clue where to begin, you're in the right place. This guide is like a parachute for people just like you, with no experience, who want to make disciples yet don't know how.

So where do we go to learn how?

The answer won't shock you: Jesus. And no, I don't mean that in the Sunday school way—like when the teacher asks what happened to the missing whiteboard eraser and the kid shoots his hand up: "I don't know, teacher, but I'm pretty sure the answer is Jesus." Because, well . . . isn't it always?

Jesus wasn't just the master disciple-maker, he was also the master trainer of disciple-makers—and he spent three years showing us how.

If you read the Gospels carefully, you see that he primarily spent more time pouring into the Twelve than he did ministering to crowds. But how did he do it? If you boil down everything Jesus did with the disciples in those three years, it comes down to three simple rhythms of disciple-making: time, teaching, and tactics.

* Time—His disciples were transformed
* Teaching—His disciples were trained
* Tactics—His disciples were sent

Here's the cool part: you can trace Jesus's three years of ministry right along those rhythms:

* In the first year, Jesus focused on spending *time* getting to know his disciples.
* In the second year, he emphasized *teaching* and training them.
* In the final year, he prepared them by giving them *tactics*, then sending them ahead.

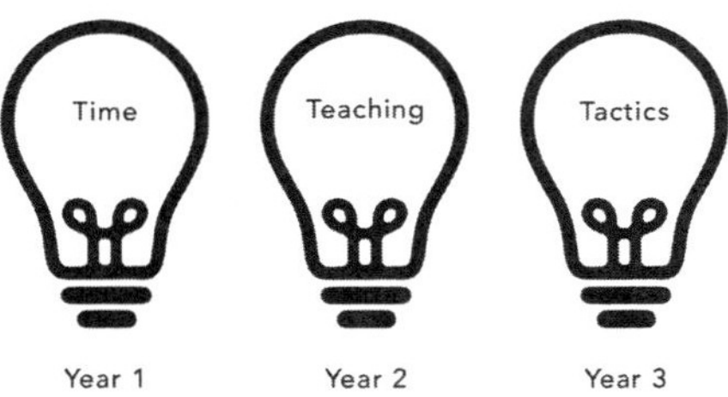

Jesus crafted an immersive experience for his disciples, with each year building on the last, forming a deliberate progression in how he made disciples. That's the heart of Discipology: learning how to walk in the rhythms of time, teaching, and tactics like Jesus did with his disciples. Trust me, it really works.

Most of us have experience with two out of three of these rhythms. On Sundays we find ourselves in the teaching rhythm, listening to preaching at church. And that's good! But you may have also entered the time rhythm in interactive small groups during the week, sharing life together. That's even gooder! But very few enter the third rhythm: tactics, learning to make disciples. And that's the goodest![2]

No matter how many of the rhythms you're walking in, they should be celebrated, because each accomplishes something uniquely different.

Teaching brings information.

Time brings transformation.

Tactics bring activation.

= DISCIPLESHIP

Combining them is where the magic happens! When you overlay the information of teaching with the transformation of time, you get discipleship.

But discipleship isn't the same as disciple-making.

Only when you overlay Jesus's third rhythm (tactics) over the first two do you get disciple-making.

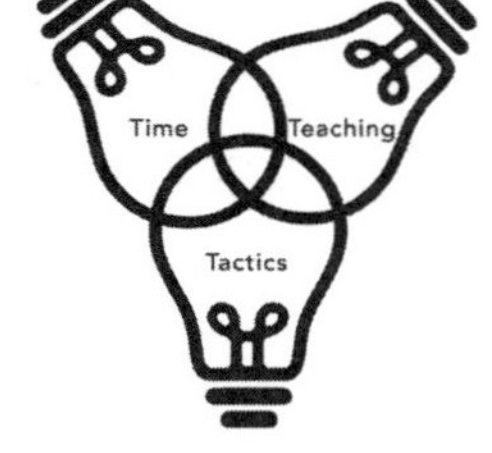

= DISCIPLE-MAKING

Now, you might like equations and formulas, but what does discipleship versus disciple-making look like in practice? And how can we distinguish between the two?

Here's Jesus's description of what *disciple-making* looks like:

> Jesus . . . said, "All authority in heaven and on earth has been given to me. Therefore go and make disciples of all nations, baptizing them in the name of the Father and of the Son and of the Holy Spirit, and teaching them to obey everything I have commanded you. And surely, I am with you always, to the very end of the age." (Matt. 28:18–20)

---

2. My bug-out bag is packed! The grammar police are banging down the door!

Let's deconstruct disciple-making into its essential ingredients:

1. Go to all nations.
2. Baptize them.
3. Teach them to obey all Christ commanded.
4. Rely on the presence and power of Christ.

Is it just me, or does Jesus's disciple-making list sound a lot more like a mission to people who *don't yet* believe, rather than instructions for Christians already in the club? *Going* to all nations. *Making* disciples because they don't yet exist. *Baptizing* them. *Teaching them to obey.* That's activation language—getting us to do stuff!

Now consider the steps to discipleship:

1. Gather fellow Christians who want to grow in their faith.
2. Pick a book of the Bible, a Christian-living book, or a small group curriculum.
3. Discuss what you read during the week.
4. Eat copious amounts of cookies, coffee cake, or donuts.[3]
5. Drink mugs of Christian crack (coffee, to the new believer).
6. Pray for a few minutes at the end.
7. Rinse and repeat for an average of six to eight weeks.

No matter how you slice it, discipleship resembles a spiritual support group, sipping Christian crack and discussing books while pounding coffee cake. And it's awesome. But adding the tactics rhythm on top of time and teaching is when we get activated on mission.

But it's kick-starting that activation rhythm that most of us struggle with. Yet if you're willing to step into the ring, we'll make a disciple-maker out of you, and teach you how to box—by helping you to get outside of it.

---

3. Nobody speaks against donuts. "Donuts. Is there anything they can't do?"—Homer Simpson, philosopher of the modern age

Pray This

Jesus, thank you for teaching me. I also want to experience transformation from being deeply involved in the lives of others by spending time with them. But Lord, if it's like sitting around a campfire, I don't want to just stay in the warmth for myself—I want others to experience it too. Teach me to walk in your rhythms of time, teaching, and tactics. Help me grow where I'm weak and take the next step with courage. Show me who needs an invitation to join me around the firelight, and give me the faith to go and get them. Amen.

Today's Time

- How were you discipled? What do you wish someone did to disciple you?
- If you're only walking in the teaching rhythm, how can you move into the next rhythm of time as well?
- Have you ever walked in the tactics rhythm before? What did you do? What did it do to you?

Today's Tactic: Narrowing Your Circle

In the last step you wrote down the names of people within your circle as your potential "who." Today the goal is to narrow the list to three. You'll eventually pick one based on their receptivity.

- Start praying today for God to narrow down the list to help you identify the person you'll invite to walk alongside you as you introduce them to Jesus.

* From your wider list, narrow down the names of three people to pursue as your "who."

My Three Potential Whos

* Continue praying for this smaller list with your "two" today over the phone or through the Discipology Plan app.

Big Idea: Discipleship shapes believers; disciple-making activates them into God's mission.

Your Lightbulb Moment —

STEP 4

Time: Becoming Disciples

After these things Jesus and His disciples came into the land of Judea; and there He was spending time with them.

—JOHN 3:22 NASB

We must use time as a tool, not as a couch.

—JOHN F. KENNEDY, "ADDRESS IN NEW YORK CITY TO THE NATIONAL ASSOCIATION OF MANUFACTURERS," 1961

Today's Teaching

So where to start? The first thing Jesus did after coming back from his temptation in the wilderness, wasn't performing a miracle, or preaching a sermon, but sharing a simple meal with two people. After John the Baptist publicly proclaimed Jesus as "the Lamb of God," John and Andrew trailed behind Jesus—curious, compelled, half-stalking, half-awestruck—trying to see what he would do next and where he was headed.

Then Jesus suddenly turned around.

"What are you seeking?" he asked. The question may have come with a wry grin, but it stopped them in their tracks. Anyone who has followed Jesus for a while knows that's a loaded question, because at the beginning of trailing behind Jesus to get a closer look, nobody really knows what they're seeking. Not fully, and not yet.

Caught off guard, they fumbled for a response. "Um . . . Rabbi, where are you staying?" It wasn't eloquent, but Jesus saw through the awkwardness of the moment. They wanted only to know more about him, but Jesus wanted them to know him (John 1:38–40).

So he extended a simple personal invitation to dinner, to talk late into the night: Come and see.

Upon accepting the invitation to the timeless act of sharing a meal, still one of the most intimate ways to get to know someone, the first two disciples embarked on the first steps of their disciple-making journey.

It's time to talk about **time**.

Your journey to disciple-making involves the three rhythms Jesus used to make disciples, and this step introduces you to the time rhythm.

They say time is a healer, but it's actually a transformer, and I don't mean a car that turns into a robot. The time rhythm produces transformation. That's why Jesus started with the time rhythm in his first year of making disciples. It's mainly social events and conversations.

Jesus demonstrated that disciple-making is not *transactional* by nature but *relational*.

That is why Jesus didn't perform a bunch of miracles, rock a mic to the masses, or grab headlines in his first year. Instead, he intentionally laid low, played it slow, stayed local, and only reluctantly did two miracles. In the Gospels, it's clear that Jesus focused solely on actions that allowed him to spend a ton of time with his new disciples that first year:

CHRONOLOGY OF JESUS'S FIRST YEAR

1 **Dinner with John and Andrew** *(John 1:39)* The first recorded moment of connection is a shared meal in the region of Perea.

2 **Calling of Peter, James, Philip, and Nathanael** *(John 1:40–51)* Jesus begins recruiting, mostly through relational networks, near the Sea of Galilee.

3 **Wedding at Cana** *(John 2:1)* Jesus brings his disciples to a wedding. He turns water into wine—reluctantly—and his disciples believe in him (John 2:11).

4 **Retreat to the Sea of Galilee** *(John 4:43–45)* After the wedding, Jesus retreats with his new disciples to decompress and bond.

5 **Trip to Jerusalem for Passover** *(John 2:13)* A festival pilgrimage leads to his first temple cleansing.

6 **Return Through Samaria** *(John 4:1–42)* A detour becomes a mission trip. Jesus shares the gospel with a Samaritan woman and spends two days with the locals.

7 **Healing in Galilee** *(John 4:46–54)* Jesus heals the centurion's servant from a distance in Cana.

8 **Settles in Capernaum** *(Matt 4:13)* He chooses this fishing village as his home base.

9 **Rejection in Nazareth** *(Luke 4:16–30)* In his hometown, Jesus refuses to perform miracles and reminds them that God's mercy often reaches gentiles first. They try to kill him.

10 **Weekend Synagogue Circuit** *(Luke 4:15)* Jesus begins preaching throughout the local synagogues in the region of Galilee, calling people to repent.

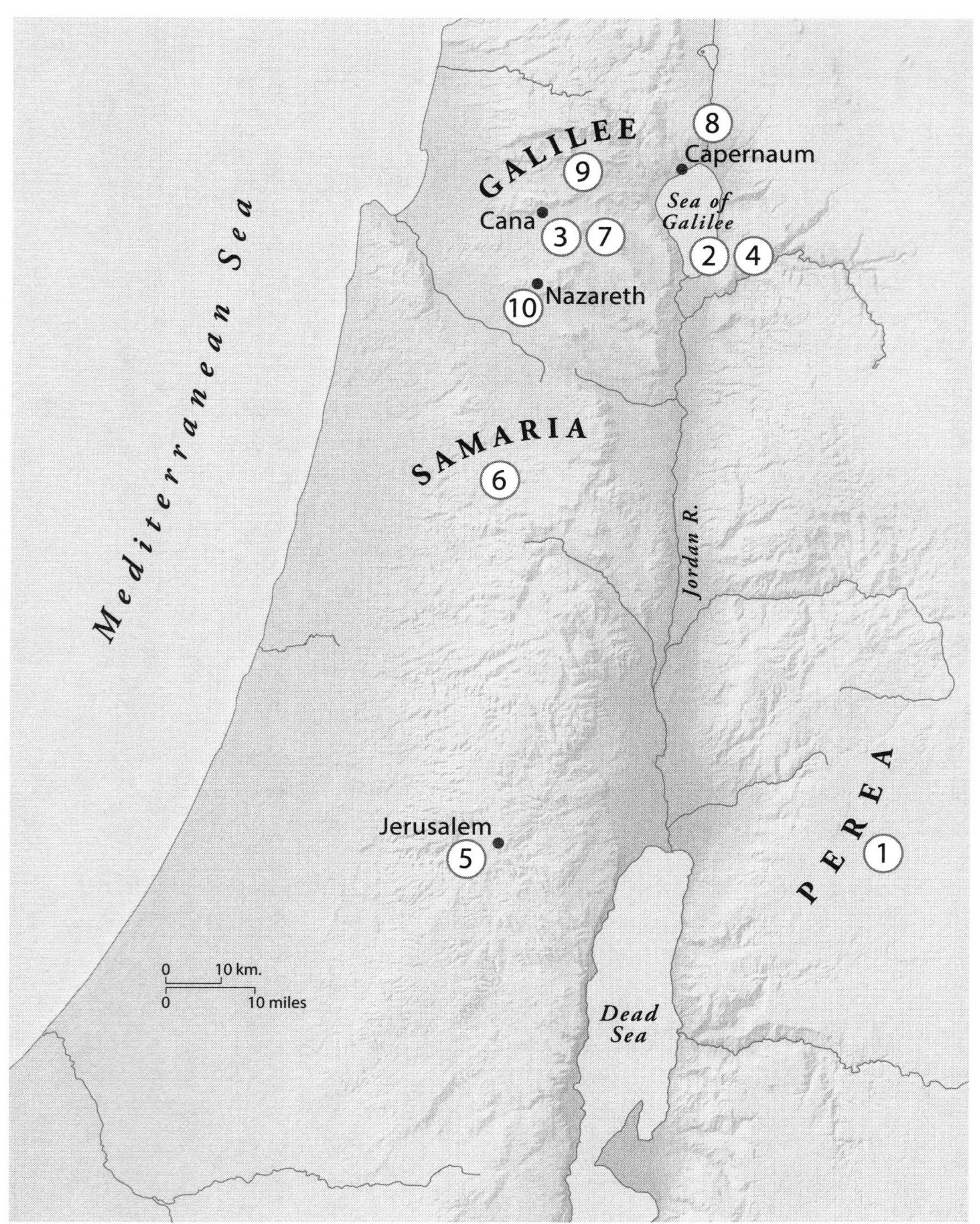
GALILEE
Capernaum
Sea of Galilee
Cana
Nazareth
Mediterranean Sea
SAMARIA
Jordan R.
PEREA
Jerusalem
Dead Sea
0 10 km.
0 10 miles
1
2
3
4
5
6
7
8
9
10

Making disciples starts with making friends and moves at the speed of relationships. This is why Jesus spent his first year simply entering the rhythms of his followers' lives—traveling with them, eating meals, attending weddings, walking along the lake. He didn't rush the process. He knew *we become like those we spend time with*. Jesus knew that if they spent enough time with him, they would become like him. And if you look at a map of Jesus's travels, over one thousand miles were clocked on the odometer. Traveling like that together—walking dusty paths, swapping stories, and huddling around the same campfire—allowed the rhythm of time to do its slow transformative work.

Sometimes the most important part of disciple-making doesn't look like much of anything at all. You're just living life together. Hanging out. Surfing. Walking your dog together. I can trace my own discipleship to a few key people who taught me how to share my faith, lead others to Jesus, pray, go on mission, and teach the Bible. But maybe more important than all those lessons was the time they gave me—doing what, at first glance, looked like *nothing*. Between those lessons, we went sailing, skateboarded down hills, ate food, and stayed up late heckling MTV—laughing until milk came out our noses. But somewhere in the rhythm of time, my life changed from the inside out just by being around them. I learned how Jesus followers speak, think, love, forgive—and yes, even fail. I saw them get it wrong too: lose their tempers, handle situations wrongly, and make bad judgment calls. That also taught me about repentance: how to humble myself, apologize, and get back up again. Transformation, it turns out, is caught, not just taught.

Back to John and Andrew. When they asked, "Rabbi, where are you staying?," Jesus didn't crack the Bible, preach a sermon, or start a debate.

He simply said, "Come and see."

Jesus didn't wait for perfect people to show up. He simply called the people right in front of him. For some reason we think disciple-making should be done with complete strangers, but Jesus showed that spending time in existing relationships is the best way to make disciples because it allows for genuine connection, trust, and influence to grow naturally over time. He harnessed the existing relationships of his first six followers. Jesus first called Andrew and John, who were friends and coworkers. Andrew fetched his brother, Peter. Philip and Nathanael were friends and most likely fished with the other four. They were friends, brothers, and coworkers.

That means relationships aren't by accident. God has put certain people in your life for a reason. The way Jesus approached disciple-making busts the two biggest myths we have about making disciples:

1. Myth #1: Disciple-making starts with strangers. (Jesus sparked a movement with existing relationships.)
2. Myth #2: Disciple-making is for lone rangers. (Jesus recruited and sent his disciples in pairs.)

Invest time in your existing relationships. Inviting a neighbor over for dinner. A coworker to a game. A classmate to coffee. That's what walking together looks like. *Time* is our most precious currency—that's why it carries so much weight when we invest it in others.

Your disciple-making plan begins by asking, *Who has God placed in my life that I could invite to spend time together?* So what are you waiting for? You don't need to know everything before you begin. People aren't projects, but if you love and value them, you're ready. Start investing time in someone today, and you'll already be taking real steps in disciple-making.

Pray This

Father, thank you for shaping me through the everyday moments and the ordinary people you've placed in my life. Help me not to rush past the slow work of transformation but to see the value of time spent walking closely with others. Open my eyes to the relationships you've already placed around me—the friends, coworkers, and family members who can help me become more like Jesus. And Lord, show me whom I can invite to walk this disciple-making journey with me. Give me courage to say, "Come and see," and grace to become someone worth following because I'm following you. Amen.

Today's Time

- Why do you think Jesus spent a lot of time with his disciples?
- Who has influenced you in the past just by spending time with you?
- What kind of margin would you need to create in your life to make time for disciple-making?

Today's Tactic: Walk Together

We all eat. That's the easiest common ground for all humans to gather around. But there are plenty of other options as well. Some of us like sports. Others like hobbies. Still more like to go to concerts.

* With your disciple-making partner, your "two," discuss an activity that the two of you could invite one of your potential "who" to. You should have six people on your list to choose from.

Big Idea: Time spent together isn't wasted—it's the gradual process that transforms us into disciples.

Your Lightbulb Moment

DATE ____ / ____ / ____

STEP 5

Teaching: Training Disciples

When Jesus had finished these words, the crowds were amazed at His teaching; for He was teaching them as one who had authority.

—MATTHEW 7:28–29 NASB

I don't know where I'm going from here, but I promise I won't bore you.

—DAVID BOWIE

Today's Teaching

The three rhythms of Jesus's disciple-making were **time, teaching, and tactics**. In the previous step, we looked at the time rhythm. Now it's time for the next rhythm: **teaching**.

Jesus's second year was all about teaching the Twelve, training them to do what he did.

Remember in the last step when I said that Jesus only reluctantly performed two miracles the first year? At Cana, when his mother asked for wine, Jesus replied, "Woman . . . my time has not yet come" (John 2:4 NLT). Woman, not Mom. Pulling the Mom card to get Jesus to do a miracle put him in a tough spot. Jesus knew that if he did miracles, the crowds would start banging down the doors leaving little time for building relationships.

But in year 2, something shifted on a dime. Jesus stepped forward with a bold announcement: "The time has come. . . . The kingdom of God has come near. Repent and believe the good news!" (Mark 1:15).

"The time has come." The quiet beginnings were over.

Right after that announcement, Jesus did a whirlwind of miracles. He cast a demon out of a man in the synagogue, healed Peter's mother-in-law, and healed all kinds of people late into the night from Peter's house. Peter and the other boys on his fishing crew were used to rising before the sun crested the hills—the best time to catch fish. Before Peter left the house, he went to check on Jesus, but he was gone. Heading outside toward the water's edge, Peter found him sitting alone with lips moving in prayer, his gaze fixed on the shimmer of the moonlight reflected on the waves.

As Peter and crew approached, Jesus startled as if pulled from another world. One of the fishermen spoke: "Everyone is looking for you." With a far-off look in his eyes, still looking across the water, in a voice low and even, Jesus said, "Let's go on to the neighboring villages so that I may preach there too. This is why I have come" (Mark 1:38 CSB).

Peter wanted to stop him, confused. Why leave now, when momentum had just begun? Jesus merely responded, "I must proclaim the good news of the kingdom of God to the other towns also, because that is why I was sent" (Luke 4:43).

Peter hadn't fully grasped what that meant. How could he? Guys like him didn't become rabbinical students. They were just fishermen. To Peter, it seemed Jesus had gathered the sorriest bunch of rabbinical students in history.

But the following day, Jesus invited them to come with him, right after the miraculous catch of fish. And Jesus's invitation came with a promise—"Follow me," he'd said, "and I will make you fishers of people."

This was a different kind of invitation from Jesus's year 1 invitation to *come and see*. Now Jesus raised the stakes from merely spending time with him. The year 2 invitation was a different kind of *follow me*—a 24/7, walk-covered-in-the-dust-of-your-rabbi kind of call.

Peter and company dropped their nets just like that. They left behind their trade as fishermen, their boats, and the life they'd known in Capernaum. With hearts pounding and eyes fixed on the rabbi who had called them, they followed him out of town.

Year 2 was Jesus's Galilean tour de force. The disciples got a front-row seat, watching as Jesus crisscrossed the region—villages, synagogues, marketplaces—teaching, healing, and announcing the kingdom. Year 2 also marked a shift in Jesus's popularity, when crowds swelled and his followers multiplied into the thousands.

And the entire time, the disciples were being trained. Year 2 wasn't about doing; it was about watching. For now, their job was to observe, absorb, and remember.

Think of *The Karate Kid*. Mr. Miyagi doesn't start Daniel with fancy kicks or fight moves. Instead, it's "wax on, wax off," "paint the fence," "sand the floor." At first Daniel thinks it's pointless grunt work. But when the moment comes, those repetitive motions kick in as reflexes—muscle memory forged through simple obedience. That's year 2 with Jesus. The disciples watched, listened, and absorbed his teaching, not realizing they were being prepared for their own disciple-making journey ahead. When the time came in year 3, what they'd learned in year 2 would surface as spiritual reflexes, their minds flashing back to what they'd learned from him. All masters know the value of training, as Yoda exhorted Luke, "Mind what you have learned. Save you it can."[1]

That entire year was the year of teaching and training for the Twelve, but it still wasn't disciple-making. For that, they'd need the tactical rhythm. That was coming in year 3, when Jesus would activate them by sending them out. For now, they were training by observing, but it was still an all-in affair. How about you? Are you ready to follow Jesus in a deeper way than just spending time with him? Are you ready to leave all you knew before? Ready to let him make you into a fisher of people?

Your first half of this journey is training, and the second half is doing. The same way Jesus prepared them, he's preparing you. Every lesson, every trial, every "wax on, wax off" action step you complete is training you for the mission ahead.

So keep your chin up, grasshopper—your Master hasn't left you unprepared. He's shaping you for what's next. One step at a time.

---

1. *Star Wars: Episode V - The Empire Strikes Back*, directed by Irvin Kershner (Los Angeles: Lucasfilm Ltd., 1980).

Pray This

Jesus, you are the Teacher I need. The Twelve didn't just hear sermons, they also watched you live the truth day by day, until it sank in. I want the same. Train me through your Word, through your Spirit, and through the small obediences of everyday life. Prepare me for what's ahead, shaping me now so I'll be ready when you send me out. Help me receive your teaching not just with my mind but with a heart willing to be formed. Amen.

Today's Time

* How does Jesus's second invitation to be made into fishers of people raise the required commitment level?
* What kind of training did the disciples receive in year 2? What teachings of Jesus have you observed and absorbed?
* What "wax on, wax off" moments in your life—seemingly small or repetitive tasks—might be preparing you for a greater mission ahead?

Scan Me

Today's Tactic: Sign Your Name on the Dotted Line

Think of your life like a check drawn from your account. Most of the time, we fill it out ourselves—deciding what we want life to look like—and then ask God to sign off on it. But Jesus's second invitation was different. He asked his disciples to hand him a blank check, already signed, trusting him to fill in the rest. They had no idea what was coming or how he would train them.

If you're ready to take the next step as a disciple-maker, you don't need to be fully prepared, worthy, or have all the answers. You just need to be willing. Are you willing to drop your nets and follow him to the next level, like Peter, John, James, Andrew, Philip, and Nathanael did that day? If so, sign your name on the following line and tell Jesus you're ready for him to take control and call the shots from now on.

Sign here . . . . **Date** . . . .

Big Idea: Training with Jesus may feel ordinary at first, but those lessons become reflexes when it counts.

Your Lightbulb Moment —

DATE ___ / ___ / ___

STEP 6

Tactics: Sending Disciples

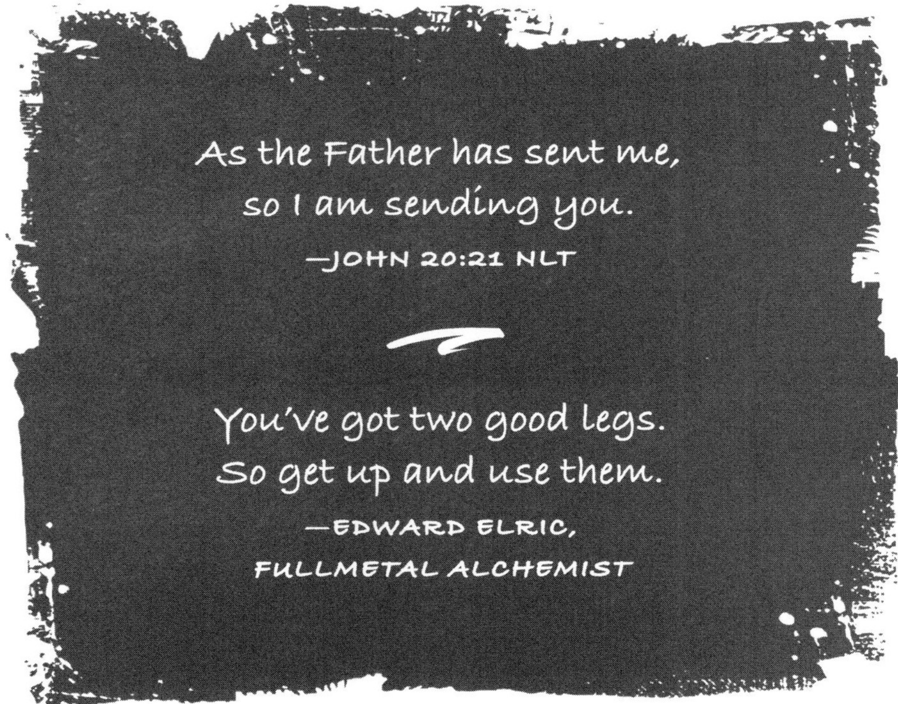

Today's Teaching

Welcome to step 6! We've covered two of the three rhythms of Jesus's disciple-making. All that's left is the tactics rhythm. But the disciples never saw it coming. Put yourself in their sandals a few thousand years ago, moments after they've learned that Jesus is sending them out on a short-term mission that would last months. This wasn't an invitation to come and see, like year 1. Nor was it an invitation to go all-in like year 2. This was an invitation to leave.

At the dawn of the third year of following Jesus, the disciples stood there wide-eyed and dumbstruck. Up until now, they had followed him like shadows, listened to his teaching, and watched miracles unfold, but this was different. Jesus's words still rang in their ears as they processed what they meant, "Do not go among the Gentiles or enter any town of the Samaritans. Go rather to the lost sheep of Israel. As you go, proclaim this message: 'The kingdom of heaven has come near.' Heal the sick, raise the dead, cleanse those who have leprosy, drive out demons. Freely you have received; freely give" (Matt. 10:5–8).

They stared at each other nervously. Was he serious? They waited for the punchline, but none came.

After walking in Jesus's dust for a whole year, they were now being sent to kick up some of their own. Did they hear him correctly? They were to cast out demons and heal the sick? Peter's jaw tightened as he scanned the horizon, wondering what kind of demons he'd face. John stole a glance at his brother James, reading the same hesitation. Matthew, still getting used to being on *this* side of the kingdom, wondered what message from a former tax collector would ever be received.

Just days before, the crowds pressed in on every side, as the sun dropped lower on the horizon. It was getting late, and someone suggested to Jesus that the people should be sent home. The disciples saw them as a problem to manage. But Jesus saw them differently. His eyes scanned the faces of the crowd—tired, hungry, restless—and his face softened. He looked at them with compassion. It wasn't just about what he saw in them but about how he wanted his disciples to see them too.

The crowd of thousands carpeted the curves of the hills like stalks of wheat, resembling a field of wheat swaying in the wind. Looking out over them, Jesus said pensively, "The harvest is plentiful but the workers are few. Ask the Lord of the harvest, therefore, to send out workers into his harvest field" (Matt. 9:37–38).

The disciples thought the workers they were praying for were other people. Instead, he was sending *them*. Sneaky trick. Classic Jesus.

And the amazing thing? None of them turned back.

Year 3 opened with Jesus sending out the Twelve and closed with him sending out the seventy-two—bookending the year with two mission trips. But in between those journeys, Jesus involved them in meaningful acts of ministry. Their hands became instruments of power. They passed out bread and fish that multiplied as they gave it, the miracle literally happening in their hands. Peter even stepped out onto the waves, and caught a fish with money in its mouth (to pay their taxes). They were no longer observers; year 3 was all about tactical activation, when Jesus flipped the switch from their discipleship to their disciple-making. And they didn't feel ready.

I'll let you in on a secret—nobody ever is.

But Jesus is ready to take you on that journey of making disciples if you're willing to enter the tactics rhythm and risk failing forward. Somebody once said, "When God designed your calling, he already factored in your stupidity." That's why your disciple-making journey doesn't start when you're ready, it starts when you say yes.

Jesus, who invented birds, pushes the disciples out of the nest, flinging them from the perch of security as if he believed that the only way people learn to fly is by flapping their wings while falling. After all, nothing activates us like action.

When I was a young youth pastor, I used to bang my head against the wall trying to follow Jesus telling the students to read the Bible, pray, share your faith, serve, come to church. I tried everything to motivate them: guilt, hype, even bribery (don't judge me). But it always felt like I was dragging them uphill in a shopping cart with square wheels.

Then one day we took them on a mission trip—and everything changed. I remember walking down the narrow cars of a bullet train speeding through Europe, seeing those same "unmotivated" kids laying hands on strangers, leading them to Christ. I could barely believe my eyes. Their gifts—hidden before—were *coming alive* right before me. It was like getting a front-row seat to a high-speed revival, and none of those kids came back the same. It didn't matter if we went to New Zealand or Mexico, the Holy Spirit turned up and wrecked these kids' worlds.

Only tactical engagement can do that. That lens brings everything else into focus.

Activating people on mission makes everything else click.

They *wanted* to read the Bible—because they needed answers.

They *wanted* to pray—because they needed power.

They *wanted* to share their faith—because real people were desperate for hope.

They *wanted* to gather—because the mission was bigger than themselves.

Faith comes alive when it's put into action. When we step into the tactics rhythm, everything changes—we don't just learn about following Jesus; we experience it. Without the tactics rhythm, Christianity is like a swimming class that never lets people get in the pool.

So here's the question: Are you ready to step into the tactics rhythm?

I know it's scary, but that's what the tactics rhythm always feels *at first*. It's like bungee jumping: your stomach is in knots, your mind races with second thoughts, and everything in you screams, "What am I doing!?" But then—you leap. And the moment your feet leave the platform, something shifts. Fear turns into adrenaline. Adrenaline turns into joy. And the first thing out of your mouth when it's over?

"Again!"

This journey to disciple-making will one day nudge you out of the nest, but first we'll get you ready, just like Jesus did with the Twelve. Here's your journey to launch:

- seven steps in the time rhythm
- seven steps in the teaching rhythm
- seven in the tactics rhythm (to practice right where you are)

And then it's bungee jumping time! You'll be sent out with your "two" to walk through the gospel of John with your "who." That's when you'll really step into making a disciple! But don't worry, you've got plenty of time and teaching to get through before that.

Pray This—

Father, thank you for everything you've been teaching me through your Word, through others, and through life with you. But I don't want to just learn about you; I want to live like you. I want to step out, trembling if I must, but trusting you to meet me in the going. Help me to be okay with being afraid. The disciples were afraid at times, but you know me well, and you know I'm no different from any of them. You know how best to activate me on your mission of disciple-making. So I trust you, Lord, and I want the adventure. If that comes with a bit of fear up front, then make me an adrenaline junkie for your kingdom! Just . . . one step at a time. Amen.

Today's Time

* How does stepping into the tactics rhythm challenge your current understanding of what it means to follow Jesus?
* Why do you think faith becomes more alive and meaningful when it's put into action?
* Think about a time when you were pushed out of your comfort zone. How did that experience help you grow? Can you use that experience to help you step out in faith before you feel "ready"?

Today's Tactic: Pray for the Journey

Before Jesus sent his disciples, he asked them to look at the fields, heads white with plump grain and ready to harvest. Then he said, "Pray that the Lord will send more workers into the field" (Matthew 9:38, my paraphrase). That's you and me, but before putting one foot in front of the others, Jesus asks us to hit our knees.

* Today, pray for the people on your combined list, and ask God to give you his heart for them. You'll be reaching out to them soon to spend time with them. So pray for opportunities to bless them and get to know them simply as people God loves and values.
* Commit with your "two" to pray regularly for every "who" on your list.

Big Idea: Don't wait until you're ready—Jesus activates you through action, fear and all.

Your Lightbulb Moment

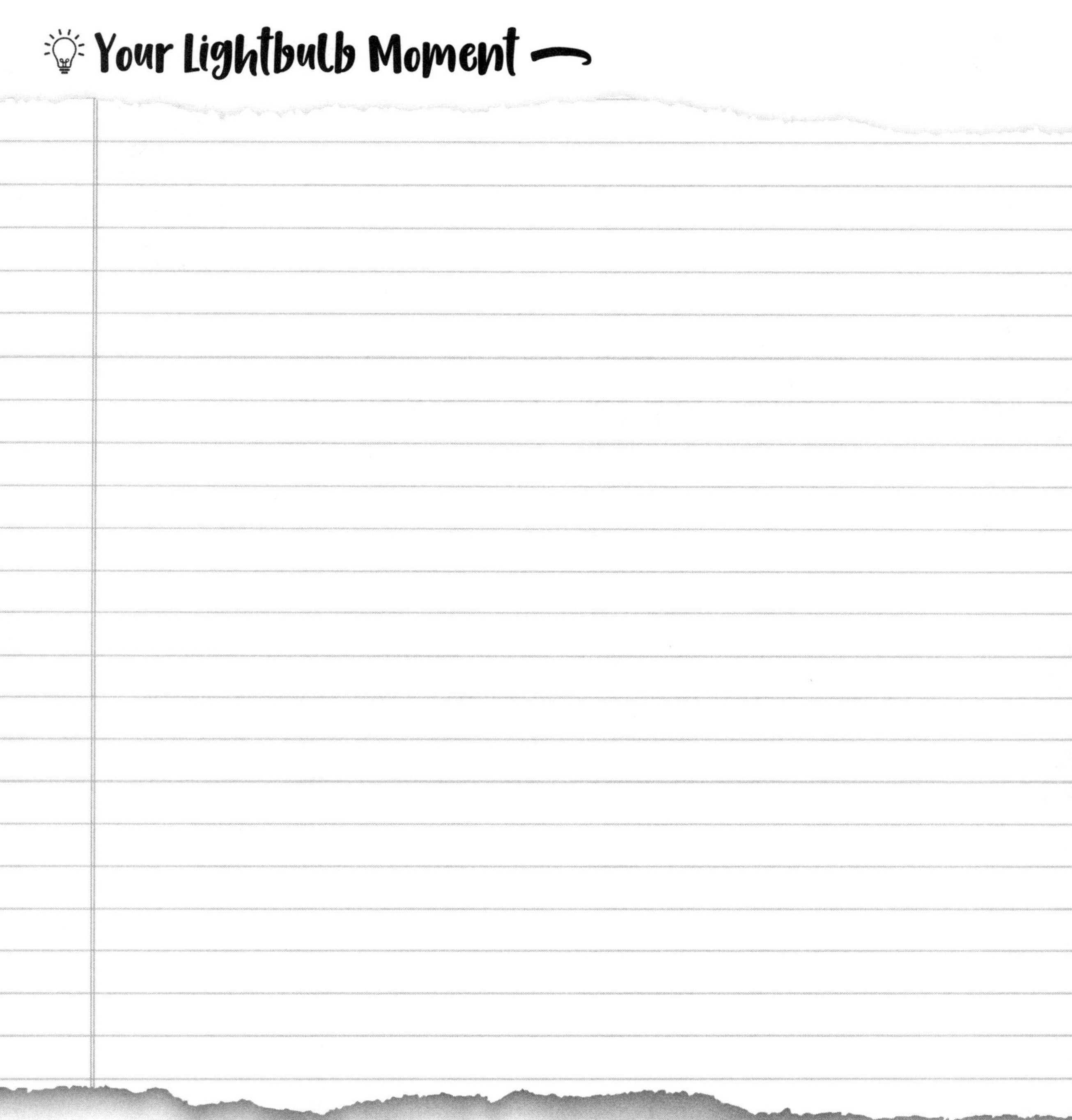

DATE ___ / ___ / ___

STEP 7

You're Not Alone

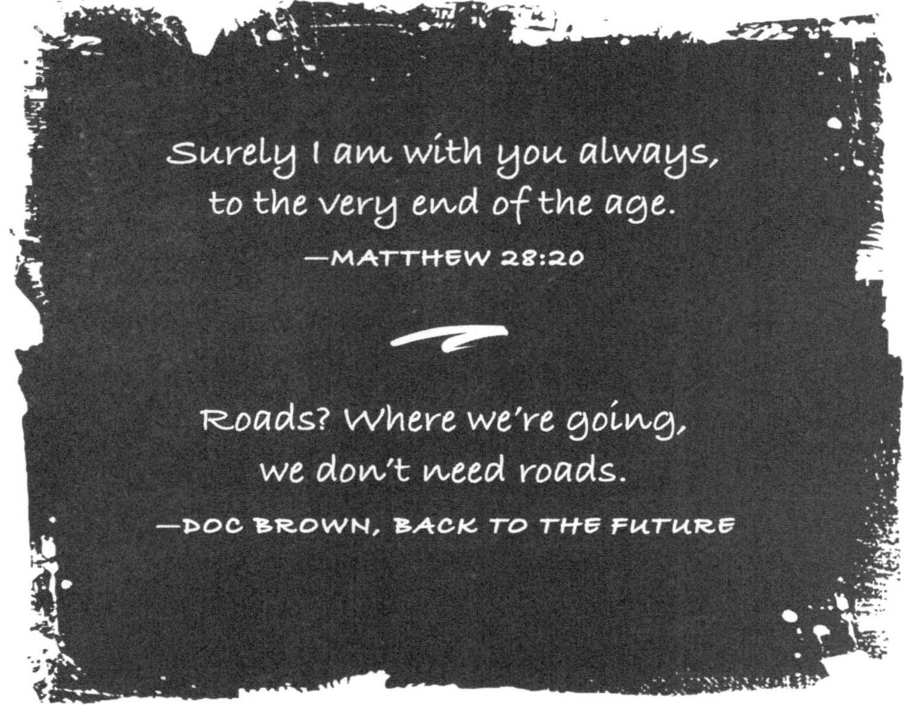

Today's Teaching

The wind stirred on the hillside in Galilee as we gathered around him one last time. We'd seen the empty tomb. We'd touched his scars. We knew beyond a doubt that he was alive. But soon he would be gone. You could feel the weight of it in the air. There was a pregnant pause as he looked around at us, like he had a year ago. We knew that look . . . we were getting sent out again.

"All authority in heaven and on earth has been given to me," he said, his voice steady, carrying across the hillside. "Therefore, go and make disciples of all nations, baptizing them . . . teaching them to obey everything I have commanded you."

Our hearts pounded. Go?

Us?

The ones who had run when he was crucified? One of us had denied him. And worse, many of us didn't believe he'd really risen from the dead at first. But then came the words that steadied us: "And surely I am with you always, to the very end of the age."

He'd already told us to wait in Jerusalem, for the promise of the Father. "You will receive power when the Holy Spirit comes on you." I don't think any of us understood at that time that he was linking his power and presence to our disciple-making efforts, but now, years later, I understand. He is still with us. It was a promise that if we go out to make disciples, he will always go with us.

You and I aren't standing on that mountain. We didn't get to see Jesus's Air Jordans airlift to heaven. So how do we know the promise of Jesus's presence is for us?

First, he promised to be with those who made disciples until *the end of the age*. Last time I checked my calendar, things were still ticking over. Second, he said to make disciples of "all nations," and the last time I looked at a map, we hadn't reached every tribe, tongue, and nation just yet. That promise was perpetual for anyone making disciples, because by now, you're starting to feel what all of us feel: "Um, God? If you're entrusting this disciple-making stuff to a knucklehead like me, I'm pretty sure you're gonna want to stay close . . ."

Jesus introduced cause for confidence with the Great Commission: "All authority in heaven and on earth has been given to me. Therefore go . . ." (Matt. 28:18–19). Jesus is saying, "I do whatever I want. I'm the one calling the shots . . . so what are you waiting for?"

He prepares people's hearts before we talk to them.

He engineers "chance" encounters.

He continues speaking to hearts long after we've ended the conversation.

God working through broken people like us is found repeatedly throughout the Bible. It proves that God doesn't use the able or qualified. He qualifies the unqualified and enables the disabled. That's the thing about fear—it whispers, *This all depends on you.* And if it did, then we'd all be sunk, and the mission would be lost. But the Great Commission wasn't a pep talk—Jesus dumping the weight of the world on our shoulders and walking away. It comes with the promise of his presence.

Instead of sending us off with, "Good luck, hope it works out." He said, "Go . . . and I'll be with you."

So whenever fear creeps in—*What if I mess this up? What if I don't say the right thing? What if I'm not enough?*—remember this: Jesus factored that into his plan already. Because if this is about his authority, his power, and his presence, then your job isn't to carry the whole weight. Your job is to trust Him.

When Paul pleaded with God to take away his weakness, the answer came back, "My grace is sufficient for you, for my power is made perfect in weakness" (2 Cor. 12:9 ESV). Instead of resenting his weakness, Paul learned to embrace it. "For when I am weak, then I am strong" (2 Cor. 12:10 ESV). Weakness was no longer his liability—but where his power lay.

You don't need to hide from your frailty or eradicate your weaknesses. You don't even need to pretend to be strong. You need to embrace your weakness, because it becomes an opportunity for Jesus to show off his strength.

Back to the disciples. Standing there, watching Jesus disappear into the clouds, the disciples pondering the gap between that Great Commission and their own inadequacy. That's why during the ten days between Jesus's ascension and the day of Pentecost when the Spirit fell on them in power, they were found praying. Prayer is a stance of weakness—a confession of inadequacy—the exhalation of surrender, followed by the intake of borrowed strength. And that's the secret: Every time we breathe out our weakness, it's replaced with the power of Christ.

So let's bring this home. We've learned what disciple-making is: following Jesus and bringing others along. We've seen who God uses: ordinary, unqualified people like Peter, Andrew, and you. We've looked at how it works: time, teaching, and tactics. And now all that's left is the obedience to go. To step out on the path in front of you. To take your "two" and begin walking with your "who."

So remember, you *don't* "got this."

Yeah, you heard me. I know people usually tell you the opposite.

You don't got this, but Jesus does. And he promised to be with you.

The disciples chose to trust those words, and they changed the world. Now it's our turn. The same Spirit is ready to guide your steps, to open doors, to engineer "chance" encounters, to speak long after you're done talking. You're not being sent alone. You're being sent with him.

Pray This

Father, thank you for being with me—always. Thank you for the power of your presence and the authority of Jesus that stands over everything in heaven and on earth. I rest in that today. I know I don't have to carry this mission on my own strength because you've already promised to go with me. Remind me that every step I take is under your authority and every word I speak is backed by your power. Help me trust that your presence is not just a comfort but the very strength I need to make disciples. Keep me close, keep me steady, and keep me moving forward in your name. Amen.

Today's Time

- How does confessing our weakness open the door for God to work powerfully through us?
- How does it feel to know that everything's not all on you?
- As you make disciples, how can you keep reminding yourself of Christ's promise of his presence and power being with you?

Today's Tactic: Pray for the Journey

Today I want you to look at your weaknesses differently—not as obstacles but as badges of honor. Think of how much glory God receives when he works through them. Your action today is simple: Don't let those weaknesses stop you. Take them to the Lord, and let him either help you overcome them, work in spite of them, or even work *through* them.

Pick one area of weakness that makes you feel unqualified—fear of speaking up, lack of Bible knowledge, insecurity, whatever it is. Write it down in the following space. Then pray Paul's prayer over it: "Your grace is sufficient for me. Your power is made perfect in my weakness" (2 Cor. 12:9, author paraphrase).

Next, write down one specific action you can take to confront that weakness, step out in faith, and do it—then watch how Jesus shows up.

Lastly, pat yourself on the back! You've made it through the first seven steps of the introduction. See you in the next seven steps, focused on the time rhythm.

Big Idea: Jesus doesn't just send you—he stays with you.

Your Lightbulb Moment

Time
Teaching
Tactics

RHYTHM 1

TIME: BECOMING DISCIPLES

For the next seven steps, we'll be focusing on the time rhythm—just like Jesus did in his first year of disciple-making. Jesus spent a year in the time rhythm before training or sending them. If he didn't rush it, why would we? So your first step is to take a deep breath and slow down. Before we can *make* disciples, we must *become* disciples. And that's what the time rhythm is all about—the slow, steady process of transformation. We go from being self-centered black holes sucking everything into ourselves, to being a people who shine his light to others.

Remember that your life is like a lightbulb. We shine God's light to others, showing them what God is like. Like the glass of a bulb, our lives are fragile and weak, but inside is the filament—the Holy Spirit—that radiates the light. When Jesus said, "remain in me" and "apart from me you can do nothing" (John 15:4–5), he meant that to shine brightly, we need to stay connected to him, like a bulb plugged into its power source. The brighter we shine, the more his Spirit transforms us from within.

So when you're fully plugged into Jesus and his power flows through you, people see through you—through the transparent bulb of your life—and see him living through you!

When Paul was searching for leaders in the church, he was looking for ordinary people whose lives showed others who Jesus is, flawed vessels showing the power of a transforming life.

And Paul didn't leave us guessing about what a transforming life looks like. He spelled it out in 1 Timothy 3:1–13 and Titus 1:5–9. The following traits describe what a mature disciple's life looks like—someone whose life looks like Jesus.

Traits of a Mature Disciple in Timothy and Titus

QUALITIES	1 TIMOTHY 3:1–7	TITUS 1:5–9
Above reproach	☑	☑
Husband of one wife	☑	☑
Not be arrogant		☑
Not be quick-tempered		☑
Sober-minded	☑	
Self-controlled	☑	☑
Respectable	☑	
Hospitable	☑	☑
Able to teach	☑	☑
Not a drunkard	☑	☑
Not violent but gentle	☑	☑
Not quarrelsome	☑	
Not a lover of money	☑	☑
Manage his own household well	☑	☑
Lover of good		☑
Not be a recent convert	☑	
Well thought of by outsiders	☑	
Upright		☑
Holy		☑
Disciplined		☑

Where did Paul get all these character traits from? Rather than making these things up out of thin air, Paul studied Jesus's life and compiled a list of character traits based on who he was and what being around him produces in our lives. These are the types of people Paul thought should lead others, but you don't have to be a church leader to be a mature disciple. These qualities should be in all our lives. At the same time, there should be things that Jesus has been getting rid of.

Marital unfaithfulness? No place for it. Arrogance? It's out. Short temper? Gotta go.

These are shortcomings that many of us struggle with, but they are areas that Jesus wants us to surrender to him. If we are going to lead others to Jesus through making disciples, it's important that they see him transforming our lives.

But true transformation doesn't happen by gritting our teeth, trying harder, and doing "gooder." So how does it happen?

Paul gives us the example of Moses, a man who met with God daily, face-to-face and, as a result, was changed. Through his encounters, Moses's face absorbed the rays of God's awesome glory like radiation, and glowed like the sun for days. It didn't take long before Moses was asked to wear a veil. Paul puts us in Moses's place: "We all, with unveiled face, beholding the glory of the Lord, are being transformed into the same image from one degree of glory to another" (2 Cor. 3:18 ESV).

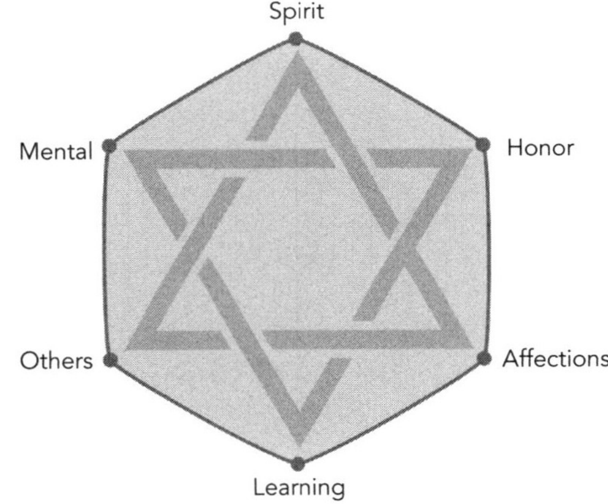

Did you catch that? Gazing into the face of Jesus transforms you, changes you "from one degree of glory to another." It's like a dimmer switch, gradually turning up the brightness in your life. That's how disciple-making works. We spend time with Jesus, following closely as his disciples, walking in the light. The people we're discipling see Christ in us and, like sailors in a storm, are drawn to him like a lighthouse.

So, over the next seven steps, we'll gaze into the face of Jesus together, looking at who he is to shape who we are becoming. That's how our character changes—not by focusing on ourselves with self-improvement, or behavior modification, or navel-gazing. If we are to see our character transform, we must start with his.

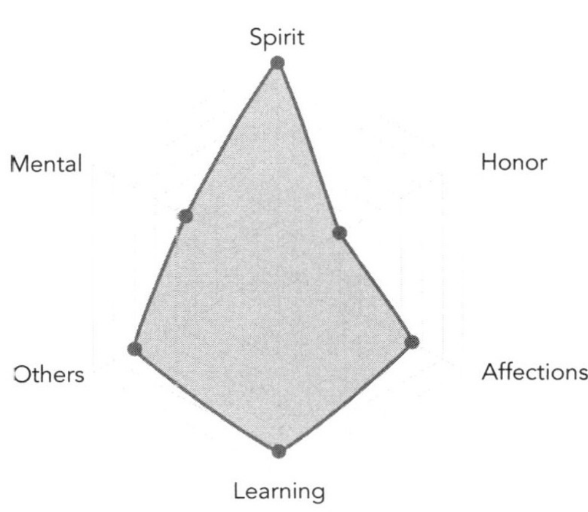

Throughout our next steps in the time rhythm, we'll use a discipleship tool called the shalom star. It's a simple assessment to help you and your "two" determine how much you're shining the character of God through your own lives. It's not a performance scorecard but a weekly checkup to spot areas that may be out of balance, and to invite God's Spirit into them.

The Hebrew *shalom* is often translated "peace," but its meaning is richer: wholeness, completeness, or a life in balance.[1] In Jesus's day, *shalom aleichem* ("peace be upon you")

---

1. Warren P. Baker and Spiros Zodhiates, *The Complete Word Study Old Testament*, Word Study Series (Chattanooga, TN: AMG Publishers, 1994), 2, 608.

wasn't just a greeting, it was a way of blessing someone with the fullness of life as the Creator intended.

The greatest commandment according to Jesus points to this wholistic integration of God into all things: "You shall love the Lord your God with all your heart, and with all your soul, and with all your strength, and with all your mind" (Luke 10:27 NASB).

- Heart: your emotional and mental life
- Soul: your spiritual life
- Strength: your physical body
- Mind: your intellect and thought life

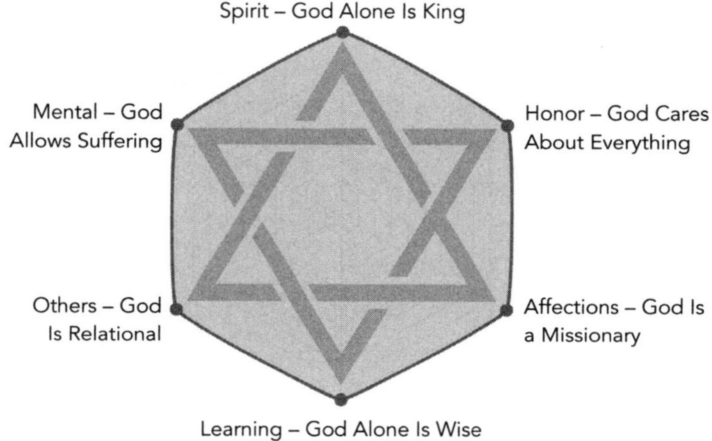

The shalom star draws from this, using SHALOM as an acronym for the areas of life brought into balance only when surrendered to God:

- **Spirit:** your soul's connection to God through prayer, worship, and Scripture
- **Honor:** your responsibilities and stewardship
- **Affections:** your family and closest relationships
- **Learning:** your intellect, creativity, and growth
- **Others:** your neighbors, community, and mission
- **Mental:** your emotional well-being and thought life

These six points also tie directly into Paul's marks of a mature disciple, which reflect Jesus. And of course, Jesus's character reflected that of the Father. He even said, "Anyone who has seen me has seen the Father" (John 14:9). Together the six points on the shalom star provide a composite picture of a life being transformed as the Holy Spirit works wholistically in every area of our lives—until we look like Jesus.

SHALOM STAR	MATURE DISCIPLES
Spirit	Holy
Honor	Respectable, self-control led
Affections	Faithful to spouse, able to manage family well
Learning	Able to teach
Others	Hospitable Well thought of
Mental	Sober minded

Over the next steps, we'll walk through each one. Transformation doesn't happen in the abstract; it happens in the everyday moments of life, step by step, day by day, because real change takes time.

So are you ready to gaze into the face of Jesus over the next seven steps? Like Moses, who left God's presence both radiant and humbled, you won't walk away unchanged. As John wrote, "Whoever says he abides in him ought to walk in the same way in which he walked" (1 John 2:6 ESV). Fix your gaze on him to be transformed, and your walk will change too.

DATE ____ / ____ / ____

STEP 8

Disciples Walk in the Light

We all, who with unveiled faces contemplate the Lord's glory, are being transformed into his image with ever-increasing glory, which comes from the Lord, who is the Spirit.

—2 CORINTHIANS 3:18

I will bring you not to the land of questions but of answers, and you shall see the face of God.

—C. S. LEWIS, *THE GREAT DIVORCE*

Today's Teaching

Learning God's character transforms our own. But of course, you knew that. You read about it in the previous few pages. Wait, what? You skipped those? Hold on there, partner . . . if we're going to change the world, we can't have you skipping parts. Go ahead and read those last few pages. Don't worry, I'll wait.

Ahem. Where was I?

The time rhythm. Jesus began with the time rhythm, not with training. Why? Because his goal wasn't merely to inform them but to form them. *Jesus cares far more for us than anything we can ever do for him.* Keep that in mind on this journey—it's like the difference between traveling economy and first class.

The time rhythm is the secret ingredient of discipleship. Therefore, it's important to clarify the difference between discipleship and disciple-making.

Discipleship is walking as a transforming disciple.

Disciple-making is walking after Jesus and bringing someone else with you.

Before we can make disciples, we ourselves must walk as disciples first. Therefore, the next seven steps focus on how *you're* transforming as a disciple, on your own discipleship journey. But remember, your own transformation never starts with you—it always starts with *God.* When God's character is revealed to us, it transforms our own. Like Moses beholding God's face, going from glory to glory, we change.

Two thousand years ago there was a man who thought he knew God better than most. His name was Saul of Tarsus. He wrote, "I was advancing in Judaism beyond many of my own age among my people and was extremely zealous for the traditions of my fathers" (Gal. 1:14). Sitting under the legendary Rabbi Gamaliel, he soaked in orthodoxy like a sponge, mastered the ancient texts of Scripture, and discerned them as windows into the very nature of God. His training completed, Saul launched out as a theological crusader, zealously defending the traditions of his fathers . . . by hunting, imprisoning, and even killing Christians.

But then Jesus appeared to Saul in a vision while he traveled on the road to Damascus, and wrecked his world. Instantly blinded, Saul realized as he crawled in the dust and shadows that he'd been *blind* about who God was all along. Worse, he'd been on the wrong road—not the one to Damascus but one to the wrong God. Saul's view of God as angry and vengeful made Saul a murderer himself. In *The Source,* James Michener captures this dynamic through the story of a grieving Canaanite woman forced to release her son to be sacrificed in a fertility ritual. Instead of comforting his wife, her husband, Urbaal, stays to "worship" with the temple priestesses. Michener writes, "She walked slowly homeward, seeing life in a new and painful clarity; with different gods her husband Urbaal would have been a different man."[1] The gods you worship determine your character as a worshiper. If you view God as angry, cold, and distant toward you, you'll reflect that to others. If you see him as gracious, loving, and humble, you'll reflect him in that way. That is why Tozer said, "What comes into our minds when we think about God is the most important thing about us."[2]

It's also why character transformation must begin with the character of God.

Saul's encounter with Jesus on the road to Damascus was his burning-bush moment—like when Moses came face-to-face with the living God—and it transformed him. Saul had known facts about God, but now he had seen his face. Blinded by the glory of Christ, Paul realized just how much he didn't know. And although Saul's sight was restored instantly at his baptism, truly seeing God for who he is took time—time spent gazing into the face of Jesus. As he learned who Jesus was, Saul changed. So much so, he changed his name to Paul, meaning small, or insignificant.

Paul termed this transformation "learning Christ," and wrote the Ephesians, "You did not learn Christ in this way . . ." (Eph. 4:20 NASB). For the New Testament definition of learning something isn't *information* but *transformation*. To learn something is to *live it*. Paul had learned who Jesus was, and it changed who he was.

Paul finally saw the big picture. God had been showing who he was all along: First, as the Father in the Old Testament, speaking through his word (Heb. 1:1); then, as the Son during the incarnation, making himself known in the flesh (John 14:9); and now, as the Holy Spirit, living within every believer and revealing himself through the church (1 Cor. 12:27).

There's a progression here: What's true of the Father, revealed in Jesus, is now expressed through the Spirit in a mature disciple.

Father

Son

Holy Spirit

Paul wanted people to see the power of the Holy Spirit's transformation working through his own life: "Imitate me as I imitate Christ" (1 Cor. 11:1, author paraphrase). As a Pharisee, Saul had been unable to change his character to reflect God. But now, as Paul, he recognized a deeper power at work within him—the Holy Spirit. He knew the Holy Spirit was transforming him from the inside out. That's why Paul consistently encouraged others to follow his example, as seen in these verses:

1. James Michener, *The Source* (Random House, 1965), 142.
2. A. W. Tozer, *The Knowledge of the Holy* (New York: Harper & Brothers, 1961), 1.

- "Therefore I urge you to imitate me" (1 Cor. 4:16).
- "Join together in following my example, brothers and sisters, and just as you have us as a model, keep your eyes on those who live as we do" (Phil. 3:17).
- "Follow my example, as I follow the example of Christ" (1 Cor. 11:1).
- "You became imitators of us and of the Lord, for you welcomed the message in the midst of severe suffering with the joy given by the Holy Spirit" (1 Thess. 1:6).

Paul is saying, "Look at me if it's helpful, but I'm looking at Jesus." We start there. Not by trying harder. Not by doing more. But by gazing at Christ. Beholding the light of his glory and letting it shine through us. Because who you gaze upon determines who you radiate to others. Over the next six steps, we'll look at six marks of mature disciples to assess how well we're reflecting Jesus and begin this journey by fixing our gaze on him.

Pray This

Father, I want to know you—not just facts about you but who you really are. Reveal your character in deeper ways, and let that revelation change me from the inside out. Shape my heart to reflect yours. Make me a person of peace, presence, and purpose because I've spent time with you. I don't want to serve out of striving or act out of pressure, but rather to live as someone being transformed by your love. Let your Spirit show me what it means to be more like Jesus every day. Amen.

Today's Time

- What do you think it means to understand God's character?
- In what ways do you think your character already reflects God's?
- What areas of your character could reflect God more clearly?

Today's Tactic: Learning Christ

The New Testament draws from the Old Testament like a deep well, including over three hundred direct quotes and six hundred allusions—all pointing to how Christ fulfilled the prophesies. When you boil down those passages, a pattern rises to the surface: six defining traits of God's character.

- God alone is king
- God is relational
- God cares about everything
- God alone is wise
- God is a missionary
- God allows suffering

The shalom star matches these character traits of God to the marks of a mature disciple. Scan the QR code to the shalom star assessment.

Big Idea: We become what we behold. Fix your gaze on Jesus, and the Spirit will transform you from glory to glory.

Your Lightbulb Moment —

DATE ___ / ___ / ___

STEP 9

Disciples Walk in the Spirit

So I say, walk by the Spirit, and you will not gratify the desires of the flesh. . . . But the fruit of the Spirit is love, joy, peace, forbearance, kindness, goodness, faithfulness, gentleness and self-control.

—GALATIANS 5:16, 22–23

Control. Control. You must learn control!

—YODA, THE EMPIRE STRIKES BACK

Today's Teaching

Welcome to step two in the time rhythm. In this step we get down to the nitty-gritty of being a mature disciple of Jesus. With the shalom star as our guide, we'll assess the first mark of a mature disciple: walking in the Spirit.

Remember, your transformation doesn't start with you but with God, so why is walking in surrender a hallmark of a mature disciple? Think back to the lightbulb. We are meant to radiate the light of who God is. The power behind that light is the Father. The light shining out is Jesus. And the filament glowing inside is the Spirit conducting that light and power through us. Without the Father, there's no power. Without the Son, no light. Without the Spirit, nothing connects.

So the question is simple: What truth of the Father did Jesus embody that the Spirit now wants to shine through you?

The answer is arrived at by breaking down what's true of each one:

The Father: God alone is king.
The Son: Jesus surrendered to his Father.
Holy Spirit: The Holy Spirit in us bows and surrenders to Jesus as King of Kings.

In summary, *Because God reigns as king, Jesus surrendered to his will so we might walk in the Spirit.*

In each step, we'll trace how this character trait of God was lived out by Jesus and now shines out of our lives by the power of the Holy Spirit. Now that you know how the sausage is made, it's time to fire up the grill.

God Alone Is King

Israel once begged Samuel for a human king: "Give us a king to lead us" (1 Sam. 8:6), but Samuel pleaded with them not to trade heaven's rule for human tyranny. They refused. From Eden onward, our bent has been to throw off God's rule and crown ourselves as the rightful rulers.

Yet the Bible begins and ends with the rule of God, opening with God ruling over creation and ending with every knee bowing. Every tongue confessing that Jesus is Lord (Gen. 1:1; Rev. 21–22; Phil. 2:10–11).

The Son Surrendered

The King of Kings stepped down from his throne in response to our rebellion against heaven's rule. Instead of striking us down, he let himself be struck for us, surrendering to death: "While we were still sinners, Christ died for us" (Rom. 5:8). His entire life was surrender. When Satan tempted him to seize power, taunting, *If you're really the Son of God . . . prove it*, Jesus remained surrendered to his Father.

Yet his disciples slowly glimpsed his kingship and authority over creation. After he stilled the storm, they whispered, "Who is this? Even the winds and the waves obey him!" (Mark 4:41). Later they watched him assert dominion over sin, death, and hell itself.

Walking In the Spirit

Let's be real: We make terrible tyrants. We say, "I'll do what I want" and hand the crown to whatever feels good—then wonder why we are soon enslaved to our desires. The truth is, we are never the ones on the throne—our appetites rule us. Deep down, we all want someone worthy to rule. Every soul wants a good king—someone to lead, protect, provide, and guide. Jesus is that king—and much better than the tyrants we settle for, including ourselves.

Instead of living only to please ourselves, we become disciples by surrendering with the confession, "Jesus is Lord" (Rom. 10:9). If Jesus is Lord, then we are not, and laying down our stolen crowns at his feet in surrender is our only response: "Offer your bodies as a living sacrifice, holy and pleasing to God—this is your true and proper worship" (Rom. 12:1), or as the NRSVue says, ". . . which is your reasonable act of worship."

But surrender is hard. It's a process. Our dethroned flesh craves control, chases comfort, and protects our preferences. But in this kingdom, God alone is king, so we surrender daily, repeatedly whispering in sweet defeat, "Your kingdom come, your will be done."

To walk in the Spirit is to recognize his exclusive right to rule, and to yield every part of our lives to him. That's why Paul describes a mature disciple as *self-controlled, not given to drunkenness, not violent, not a lover of money*—like Jesus. Therefore, these are qualities of a life that is surrendered to Jesus as Lord, a disciple who is walking in the Spirit.[1]

FATHER	SON	HOLY SPIRIT
God alone is king	Jesus surrendered his will to God	So we can walk in surrender to the Holy Spirit

1. Paul also lists out the contrast between walking in the flesh versus walking in the Spirit in Galatians 5:16–26.

Pray This

God, I want to surrender—not just part of me but all of me. Help me let go of control, of pride, of the desire to rule myself. Teach me to trust you with everything, especially the things I can't fix or understand. You are a good king. You gave everything to rescue me. Shape me into someone who follows you with open hands and a willing heart. I surrender to your loving and rightful rule over my life. Your kingdom come. Your will be done. Amen.

Today's Time

The shalom tool assesses whether we're living in harmony with God's design. This step will help you assess how you walk in surrender. Spiritual health is less about how much we're doing for God and more about how closely we're walking with him. Are we resting in him? Listening for his voice? Yielding? Jesus cultivated intimacy with the Father—stepping away to pray, resisting sin's pull, and recentering on his mission. That's the blueprint for us. As you use the shalom assessment, remember that it's not about achieving righteousness—Jesus already did that for you. It's about recalibrating your spiritual life so every part of you—mind, body, heart, and soul—stays aligned with him.

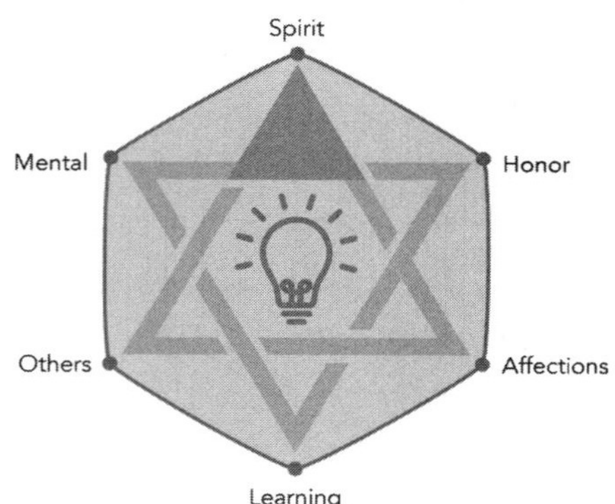

- ✱ Share your shalom assessment score with your two.
- ✱ What does walking in surrender mean to you?
- ✱ What areas are difficult for you to surrender to God? Why?
- ✱ What steps can you take to recognize his right to reign in that area?

Today's Tactic: Mini Fast

Jesus fasted. Crazy, right? Why would he do that? Fasting is the practice of giving something up in order to redirect your full attention to God. There is also no set length of time required for fasting. While the sun is shining? A week? An afternoon? Perhaps try fasting from something you rely on or something that distracts you. It could be your phone if that is keeping you from prayer. It could be alcohol, shopping, or food. Whatever you decide to do, make it yours and have fun. Fasting should be like going on a date with God where you give him more attention than usual—and more of yourself.

Big Idea: Walking in the Spirit means surrendering—because the Father reigns as king, the Son bowed to his will, and now the Spirit bends our lives to shine his rule through us.

Your Lightbulb Moment

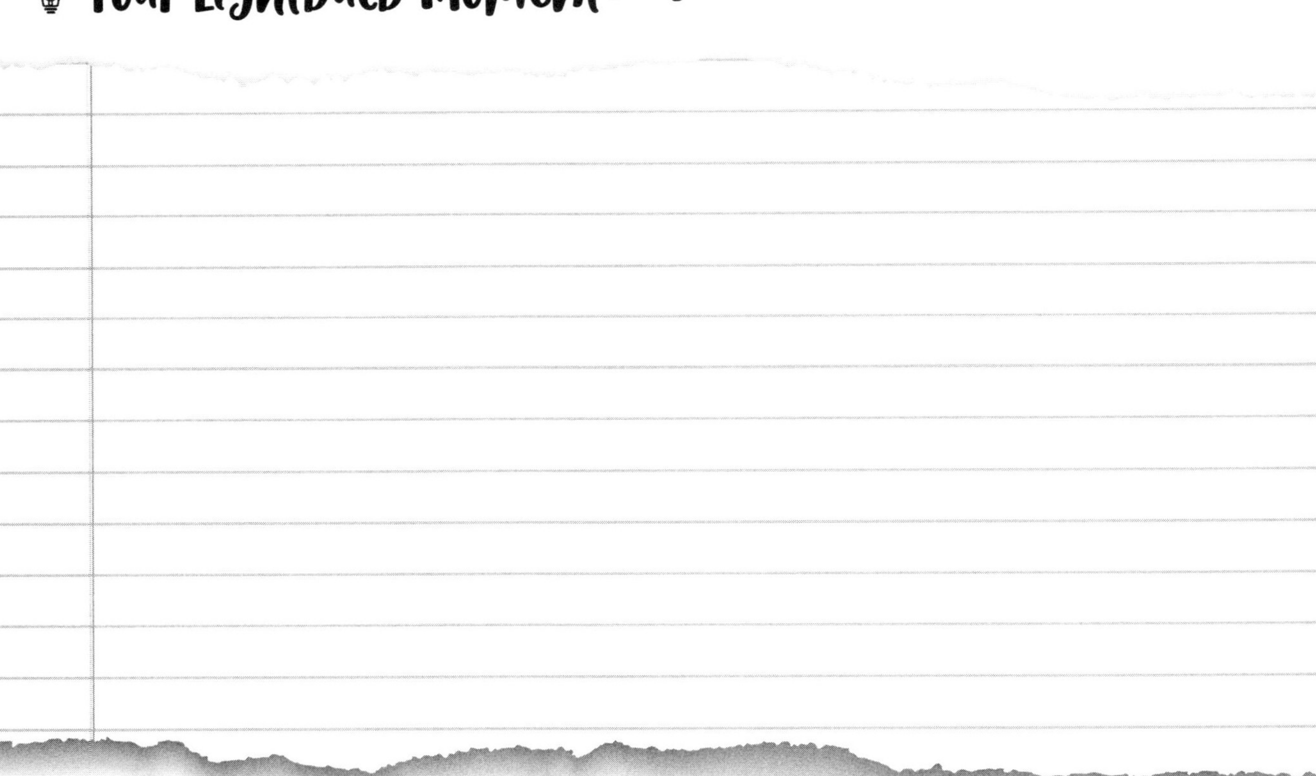

DATE ___/___/___

STEP 10

Disciples Walk Honorably

Whatever you do, work at it with all your heart, as working for the Lord, not for human masters.

—COLOSSIANS 3:23

My mama says you have to do the best with what God gave you.

—FORREST GUMP

Today's Teaching

So far we've covered one mark of a mature disciple—that we are to walk in surrender, which is what Paul calls walking in the Spirit. Today we'll learn what it means to *walk in honor.*

A mature disciple honors their responsibilities, faithfully stewarding whatever God entrusts to them. And when we honor the responsibilities in front of us—work, family, promises, even the small unnoticed things—the light of Jesus shines out of us and the character of God shines through us. We reflect a God who cares. When I was young, I took seriously the command "Whatever you do, work at it with all your heart, as working for the Lord" (Col. 3:23). My bosses always took notice and wanted to know why I worked as hard as I did. That became my opportunity to share that I was *working as worship.*

Who God Is

The God of the Old Testament wove himself into every part of life: work, worship, family, rest, and celebration. The way the Israelites talked, the way they worked, how they treated their animals, and how they rested on weekends all mattered to him. Everything mattered, even the mundane. Jesus summed it up simply: Every command boiled down to loving God and loving others. That love was to blend into every area of life. The Law was really *The Idiot's Guide to Loving God and Loving People.* And when God cares about everything, the mundane becomes monumental. Meaning integrity matters in the little things, including how we treat the land, how we talk to our neighbors, and how we work. We're to walk honorably in each of the responsibilities God gave us to steward.

Who Jesus Is

Jesus cared about the little things and honored his obligations. At the wedding in Cana, he quietly turned water into wine, at the request of his mother, saving his family friends from embarrassment. His first public sign being something so mundane—ensuring the wine didn't run out at a wedding—proved that God delights in every part of life, even the small, ordinary, and seemingly insignificant things. Even from the cross, Jesus honored his obligation to his mother, entrusting her to John's care (John 19:26–27). Jesus modeled what it looks like to steward relationships and responsibilities faithfully.

Hmmph . . . Jesus was a good son. Maybe you should call your mom. Just saying . . .

Who We Are

So what does walking honorably look like in a mature disciple?

Paul told the Thessalonians, "Make it your ambition to lead a quiet life: You should mind your own business and work with your hands, just as we told you, so that your daily life may win the respect of outsiders and so that you will not be dependent on anybody" (1 Thess. 4:11–12). In other words, take care of your responsibilities. When Christians neglect the ordinary parts of life, it stinks up the witness of the gospel.

That stewardship includes taking care of our bodies. Paul wrote, "Do you not know that your bodies are temples of the Holy Spirit, who is in you . . . ? You are not your own; you were bought at a price. Therefore honor God with your bodies" (1 Cor. 6:19–20). There's that word again—*honor*. Daniel ate healthy. Jesus took naps. Even physical training, Paul said, "is of some value" (1 Tim. 4:8).

Mature disciples know that the mundane matters matter to God. In 1 Timothy 5:18, Paul quoted an odd Old Testament law: "Do not muzzle an ox while it is treading out the grain." Random? Not really. Paul applied it to real life: If God cares about how we treat an animal, how much more should we care for people? If the little things matter, then everything matters.

So how are you stewarding your responsibilities? What conclusions are drawn by those outside the faith when they drive past a believer's house where the lawn isn't mowed, the roof isn't repaired, and the cars are never washed? It shows that something is unbalanced.

That's where the old criticism comes from: "They are so heavenly minded that they're no earthly good." C. S. Lewis countered the old jab, saying, "If you read history you will find that the Christians who did most for the present world were just those who thought most of the next."[1] That means that instead of shirking their responsibilities, they stewarded them with an eternal perspective.

It's why Paul's list of the marks of mature disciples who lead others includes *loves what is good* and *respectable*. Your life can show that if God cares about the little things, certainly he cares about other people and their lives too. If the *walk honorably* step had a bumper sticker, it wouldn't be "Dance like no one is watching." It would say "Work like it's worship—because everyone's watching." And trust me, they are.

FATHER	SON	HOLY SPIRIT
God cares about everything	Changed water to wine	So we can walk in honor

1. C. S. Lewis, *Mere Christianity* (New York: HarperOne, 2001), 134.

How to Measure Honor

Honor is about reputation, but it's also about wholeness. Stewarding what's been entrusted to us starts with discipline and integrity, and it radiates outward in how we handle our responsibilities.

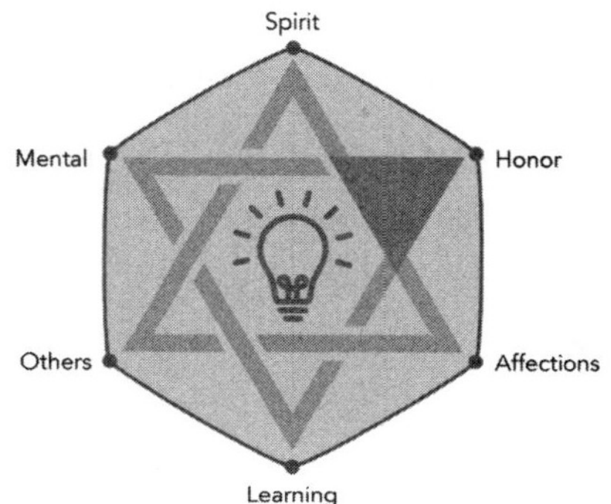

Pray This

God, help me take my responsibilities seriously, knowing that you see everything and care about it all. Starting with my laxed responsibilities, I bring them to you, casting my care upon you, for I know you care about me. Teach me to work with diligence, to pursue excellence even in the smallest things, and to live each day as an act of worship. When I'm tempted to cut corners, give up, or do the bare minimum, remind me that I'm serving you, not just people. Shape my attitude so that my actions reflect you as a God who cares—not just for me but for them too. Amen.

Today's Time

* How does diligence in small things reflect God's care for everything? How does being lazy or deceitful misrepresent him to others?
* What current responsibilities do you need to steward?
* What is one step you can take to grow in honoring what's been entrusted to you?

Today's Tactic: Do It Well

You've heard Nike's slogan "Just do it," right? Give yourself a new motto: "Just do it *well*." (I know, it doesn't roll off the tongue.)

Today give something your best: Tidy a space, send a thoughtful email, finish a chore you've been putting off.

Do it with care and excellence, knowing that God sees it and others do too. Talk about a tangible effect of your faith on the world around you!

My responsibility I'll honor this week: ______________________________

Big Idea: A mature disciple treats even the smallest responsibilities as worship, because if it matters to God, it matters to us.

Your Lightbulb Moment

STEP 11

Disciples Walk in Affection

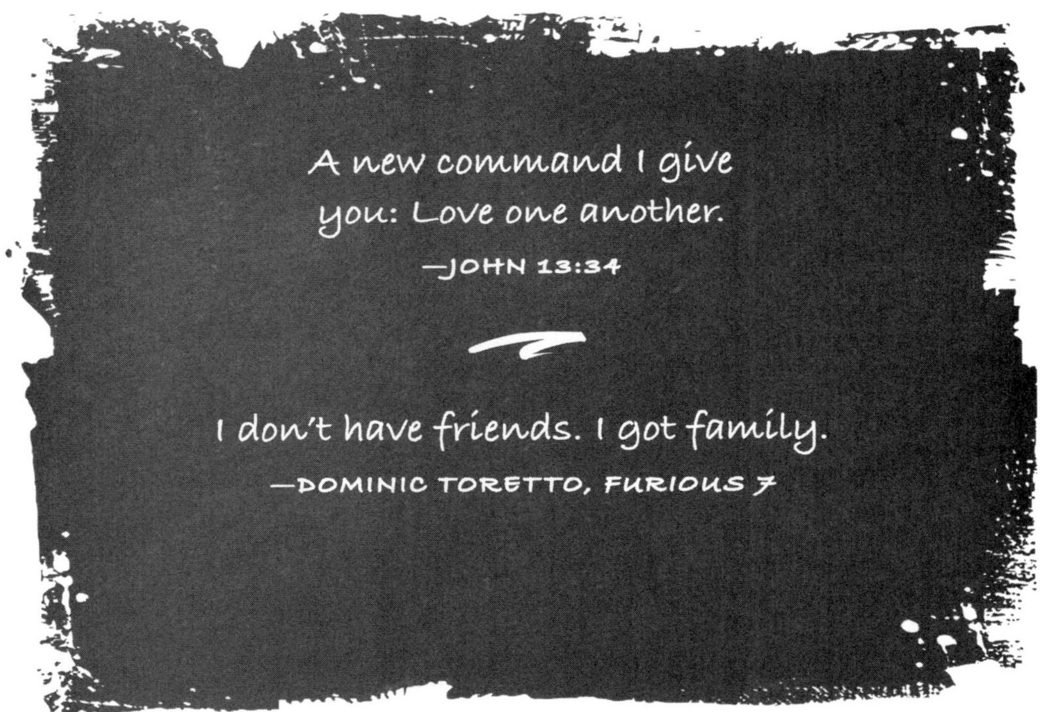

Today's Teaching

We've learned so far that on our discipleship journey Jesus transforms us to walk in surrender to the Spirit. He also transforms us so that we walk in honor, stewarding our responsibilities because everything, even the little things, matter to him.

But here's the tension: It's impossible to walk in surrender and honor your responsibilities and still neglect your family. Too many disciple-makers have focused on winning the hearts of the world outside their doors while starving the hearts at home.

Once again, transformation always begins with God and who he is rather than who we are. Because God is love, we walk in affection, beginning with those closest to us. Paul put it plainly: "Walk in the way of love, just as Christ loved us" (Eph. 5:2).

That love must begin at home. If our discipleship doesn't touch the people under our own roof, it's not the real thing. The affection we show in the everyday moments with our family—patience, kindness, forgiveness—is the same love we extend to the family of God and carry out into the world. That's how disciples walk: in the loving affection that reflects the Father's heart.

Who God Is

How do we know that God is *love*? God exists as the Trinity—Father, Son, and Holy Spirit—in a perfect, eternal bond of love. Before anything was created, God already had community, connection, and affection. So when he made us, it wasn't to fill a hole or cure his own loneliness. It was to invite us into the relationship he already enjoyed. That's why we're wired for connection, with God and with each other.

Paul says, "I kneel before the Father, from whom every family in heaven and on earth derives its name" (Eph. 3:14–15). Our families on earth are meant to be a glimpse of the Father. Every good relationship reflects him.

You can see this characteristic from our beginnings in Eden, when God walked with Adam in the cool of the day, strolling beside him like a friend. Abraham was called a friend of God (2 Chr. 20:7; Isa. 41:8; James 2:23). Moses spoke with him "face to face, as one speaks to a friend" (Ex. 33:11). We were made to know him and to make him known. God is a relational being.

Who Jesus Is

Fast-forward to Jesus's baptism, and the Father, Son, and Spirit are all present: the Son rising from the water, the Spirit descending like a dove, and the Father declaring his delight. It's less ceremony than family reunion, with God's relational heart on display.

And although Jesus loved his earthly family, he expanded the concept to include spiritual family, widening the circle. When his mother and brothers tried to pull him away from a crowded house, he asked, "Who is my mother, and who are my brothers?" Then he pointed to his disciples: "Here are my mother and my brothers. For whoever does the will of my Father in heaven is my brother and sister and mother" (Matt. 12:48–50). In that moment, Jesus revealed what his church would become—an adoptive family.

Who We Are

Paul said that before a disciple could lead anyone else, "he must manage his own household well . . . for if someone does not know how to manage his own household, how can he take care of God's church?" (1 Tim. 3:4–5 NRSVue). Walking in affection starts under the roof of a disciple-maker before going out the door. Leading someone to Jesus is great, but if done at the neglect of leading your children, something is unbalanced. Our homes are meant to shine out the love of Jesus to others. People should be curious about our families and why there's so much love in our relationships. In Paul's list marking mature believers, he includes *being faithful to your spouse* and having *children who believe*. The first disciples God ever entrusted you with are your kids, and the first ministry we all have is to our spouses.

Disciple-makers need to be good at building relationships outside of their families. That's why Paul didn't address Timothy as "my dear ministry intern" but as "my true son in the faith" (1 Tim. 1:2). As a mature disciple himself, Paul walked in affection with the disciples he made. That said, something is off if you treat your family like garbage while out there trying to be everybody else's best friend. Entire generations got that wrong, but way back in the beginning, Paul had his eye on it. He said to start at home. Start with the people around you. Your parents, your spouse, your kids. Your family.

Love them first and love them well.

Then go save the world.

FATHER	SON	HOLY SPIRIT
God is love	Jesus channeled the Father's love to the world	So we walk in loving affection

Pray This

Father, help me reflect your heart by being present, patient, and loving toward those around me. Teach me to see others the way you see them, to value relationships the way you do, and to build others up instead of pulling away. Soften any pride or frustration in me and replace it with humility and compassion. When I'm tempted to isolate myself or argue, remind me I'm part of a family, one built by grace. Most of all, help me listen and love well, to listen to you and the people you've placed in my life. Help me to be a conduit of your love to people who desperately need it as much as I do. Amen.

Today's Time

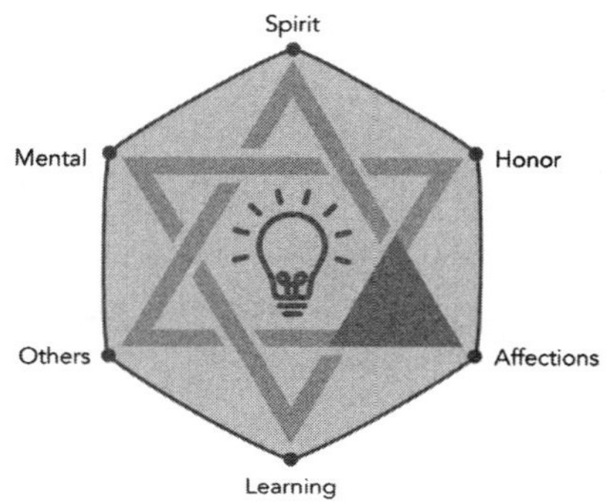

This part of the shalom star helps you consider whether the people closest to you experience your transformation. Do your closest relationships reflect God's love—not perfectly but in grace, humility, and consistency? When your inner circle of family and friends experience the love of God through you, it creates ripple effects that extend far beyond your walls and into the disciples you make.

- Share your shalom assessment score with your two.
- In your own words, what does it mean for God's love to flow through your affections?
- Are you showing patience, kindness, and forgiveness to your family, reflecting God's love in your everyday interactions?
- What do you think is the most difficult part about being loving, and what practical steps can you take this week to love the people closest to you well?

Today's Tactic: Focus on Your Family

All relationships take work. Without a little TLC, all relationships drift apart, grow tense, or become unfulfilling. So today, pick a close relationship in your family or inner circle of friends and do the following:

- Seek to love them with the deep love of Jesus. Send them a note of encouragement during the day. Perhaps surprise them with a gift, flowers, or a DoorDash treat as an embodiment of the grace you've been striving to show others outside your circle.
- Write a reminder every week to repeat this behavior, then continue to add one more person for the next few weeks until it becomes a habit.

Big Idea: Discipleship that skips your own family isn't real—love starts at home and ripples outward.

Your Lightbulb Moment

DATE ____ / ____ / ____

STEP 12

Disciples Walk as Learners

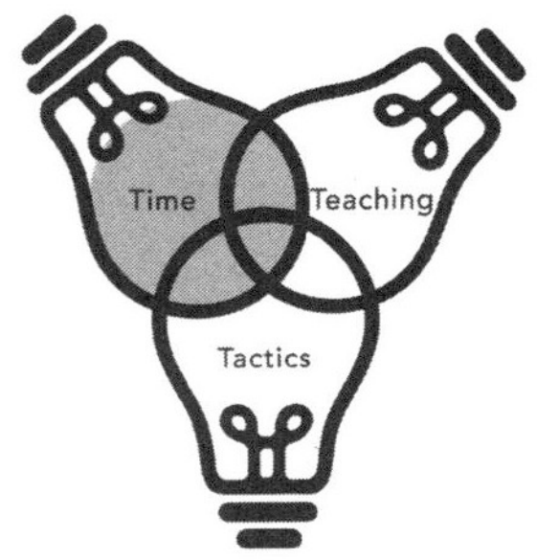

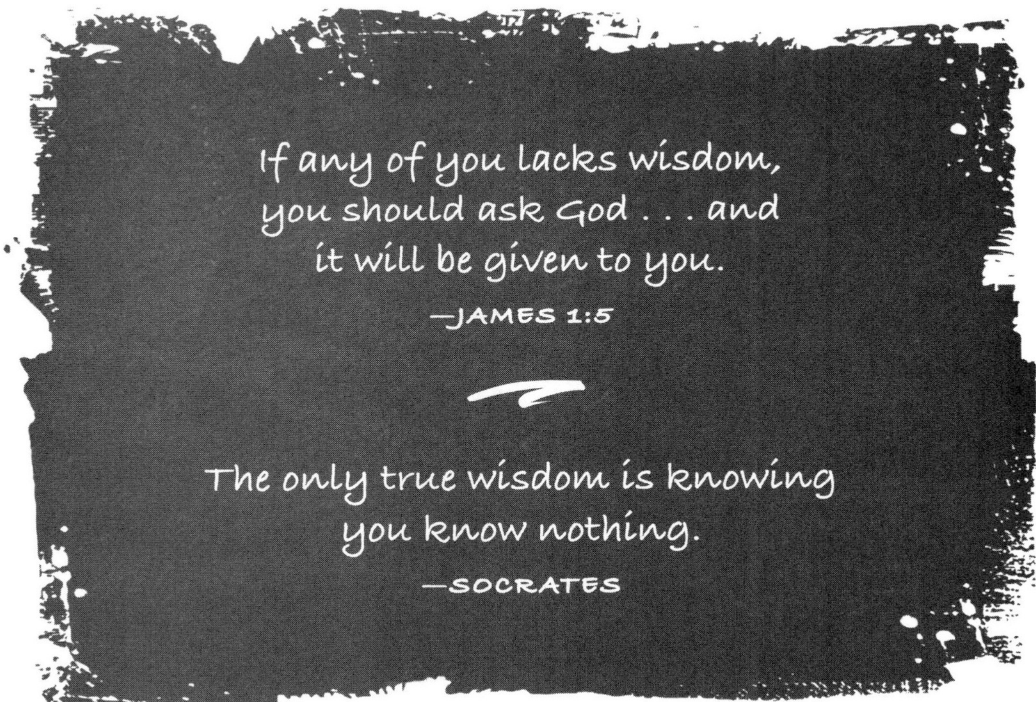

Today's Teaching

We're halfway round the shalom star now. Three points down and three to go.

This step talks about walking as learners—where God transforms our minds. The Bible teaches that God alone is all wise and the source of all wisdom. That means that a mature disciple adopts the posture of a lifelong learner. After all, *disciple* literally means "a student or learner."

I've got some news for you: You don't know everything. Worse still, you don't even know how much you don't know. And if you've ever tried to teach someone who thinks they know everything, it's a lost cause. It's like using GPS but second-guessing the route. The directions tell you to take the long way, and you're like, "No way. I know the faster route." But what you don't know is that a poultry truck flipped over on the freeway, and now there's a smoldering chicken apocalypse clogging every lane. (This actually happened to me on the way to San Diego Comic-Con. I ignored Siri and paid the price—four hours trapped in a panicked, feathery, Kentucky-Fried traffic jam.)

Trusting the wisdom of God's GPS sometimes feels counterintuitive. His directions zig-zag, when according to our own understanding, a straight line would do. Only later, glancing in the rearview, do we glimpse his wisdom. Mature disciples learn to stop arguing God's guidance, knowing that maintaining the posture of a learner is essential. Because God is all-wise, Jesus pursued wisdom, so through the Spirit mature disciples walk in learning.

Who God Is

Job understood this the hard way. His story—arguably the oldest written book in the Bible—centers on God's silence in our suffering. After thirty-seven chapters of Job asking, "Why, God?," and his friends' attempts at filling the silences, God finally responds with . . . more questions.

"Where were you when I laid the earth's foundation? Tell me, if you understand." (Job 38:4)

"Have you ever given orders to the morning, or shown the dawn its place?" (Job 38:12)

"Have you entered the storehouses of the snow or seen the storehouses of the hail?" (Job 38:22)

"Can you bind the chains of the Pleiades? Can you loosen Orion's belt?" (Job 38:31)

In other words, I don't owe you an explanation, Job. Bring the receipts. Spoiler alert: Job came up empty.

What Job discovers isn't a clear, satisfying answer—that would be information. What Job needed from an all-wise God was wisdom—wisdom to trust when no information was forthcoming. And trust works only when you know you don't know everything. You and I are allowed to ask questions. That's what makes us human. But faith grows when we choose to trust even when we don't get the answers - trust in a God who knows what we don't - in a God who sees what we can't.

I don't know about you, but my inner Job gets loud sometimes. "Come on, God—try me. I'm sure I could handle the plan if you just explained it better." But mature disciples are learners, and truly learning sometimes means being content with not knowing.

Who Jesus Is

At twelve years old, Jesus was already seeking wisdom like Solomon. After three panicked days, his parents found twelve-year-old Jesus in the temple "sitting among the teachers, listening to them and asking them questions" in the listening posture of a learner (Luke 2:46).

And here's something that might surprise you: Jesus also didn't know everything. He said there are some things only the Father knows (Mark 13:32). Limiting himself as a man, he trusted his Father's wisdom to guide him step-by-step, modeling the learning posture of a mature disciple.

Who We Are

And now us. Loving God with your mind is part of the Great Commandment: "Love the Lord your God with all your heart and with all your soul and with all your strength and with all your mind" (Luke 10:27). God wants your head as much as your heart. He invites us to think deeply, wrestle honestly, and study diligently. And thinkers like R. C. Sproul, Timothy Keller, Martyn Lloyd-Jones, J. R. R. Tolkien, Flannery O'Connor, Charles Spurgeon, Dorothy Sayers, Madeleine L'Engle, and C. S. Lewis loved and glorified God with their reason, creativity, and intellect.

A maturing disciple doesn't stop at belief but presses into understanding, aiming not merely to know *about* God but to think like him too. Rather than bypassing our mind, the Spirit transforms it, renews it (Rom. 12:2). He also tells us to "take captive every thought to make it obedient to Christ" (2 Cor. 10:5). That means that disciplined thinking is a mark of a mature disciple.

This doesn't mean you have to be a brainiac. Paul's list of the traits of mature disciples includes *able to teach*. We don't have to be eloquent or clever, just able to share what God has already said. And to do that, we must "study to show [ourselves] approved" (2 Tim. 2:15 KJV). Because the wisdom isn't ours, it's his.

Throughout the Bible, Jesus's disciples were almost always on a "need to know" basis. On the night before the cross, they finally said, "Now you are speaking clearly" (John 16:29). But by the next day, they were scattered and confused again. Following Jesus will feel like that sometimes. Clear one moment, cloudy the next. But trust his wisdom always, because you don't have to know everything. You just need to trust the One who does.

FATHER	SON	HOLY SPIRIT
God is all-wise	Asks questions in the temple	We walk in learning

Pray This

Father, help me to love and worship you with my mind. Help me to grow in knowledge while also understanding the limitations of knowledge. I don't always understand what you're doing, but I want to trust that you see what I can't see. When chasing answers doesn't work, I want to just start seeking you. Give me a heart that longs for wisdom more than comfort or control. Teach me to walk by faith, not by sight and to believe that your way is better, even when I don't get it. Lead me with your wisdom and steady me with your presence. Amen.

Today's Time

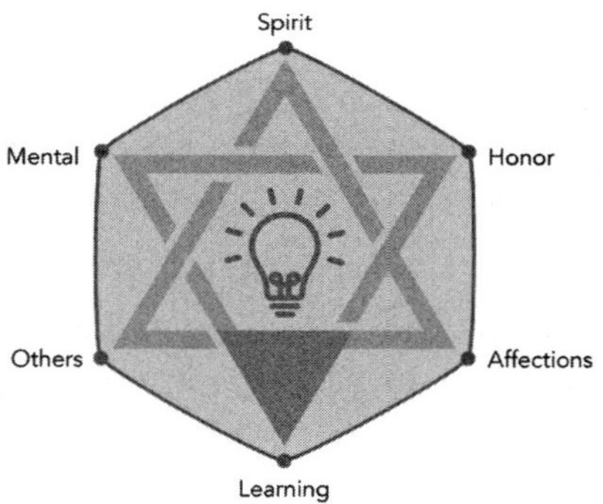

How do we measure whether we're walking in learning—that our minds are being transformed and renewed? It's often about our posture. Learning isn't automatic, it's pursued. We are told to pursue wisdom. Peter tells us to "make every effort to add to your faith goodness; and to goodness, knowledge" (2 Peter 1:5) For this reason, A. W. Tozer read Shakespeare on his knees, begging God to give him light from wherever he could find it. The shalom star measures how we're pursuing wisdom, listening to others, reading, asking good questions, growing in wisdom (Luke 2:52), stretching our mind, and deepening our understanding. Not to stockpile knowledge for pride's sake but to better reflect God's wisdom in the world.

- Share your shalom assessment score with your two.
- What do you think is the difference between knowledge and wisdom? How might the pursuit of each help you love God with your mind?
- In what area of your life do you need to trust God for wisdom when you don't have information?
- How are you growing in the wisdom of God through the Word of God?

Today's Tactic: Say a Little Prayer

Jesus prayed to seek God's wisdom, and so should we.

- Take a few minutes to ask God for wisdom in an area where you feel unsure or anxious. Write down what comes to mind, even if it's just a sense or a Scripture. Then, decide to trust him with what comes next, even if you don't fully understand it.
- Pursue wisdom and start a Bible habit, pick up a book, or educate yourself on something you've been putting off because it seems like too much work. Simply read for five minutes a day.

Big Idea: A mature disciple stays a learner, loving God with their minds but also trusting God's wisdom when answers don't come.

Your Lightbulb Moment

STEP 13

Disciples Walk with Others

How beautiful . . . are the feet of
those who bring good news.

—ISAIAH 52:7

I made a pilgrimage
to save this human race

—MODERN ENGLISH,
"I MELT WITH YOU"

Today's Teaching

Because God is a missionary God, mature disciples walk with others: walking with insiders to reach outsiders.

Think of it this way: *We walk with our "two" to reach our "who."*

But of course, you know this. God is a missionary God who never sends us out alone, but rather sends us with others to reach others. Withness as witness. Mission itself is relational, which explains why disciple-making is based on relationships.

Unfortunately, this clashes with many of our childhood dreams. As kids, many of us wanted to be Batman or Batgirl—a Dark Knight, the lone vigilante—saving the world by grit and determination. But our dreams of being the self-sufficient hero, the 007-type agent who works alone, is fiction.

Who God Is

From his very first breath in Eden, Adam woke up alone. But the voice of a missionary God spoke about others: "It is not good for the man to be alone" (Gen. 2:18). So why create Adam solo in the first place? To teach him that he needed a "two." Once placed in a partnership, Adam and Eve were given their mission to "be fruitful and multiply" (Gen. 1:28 ESV).

That pattern runs through the whole Bible—every mission is shared. Why? Because it mirrors our missionary God himself—the Father, Son, and Spirit an eternal community on mission, reaching out in love.

The pattern continued with a pagan named Abram. God is a missionary God, so he started by reaching out to an outsider—someone other. From Abram, God would build a community on mission, echoing his relational heart, a nation to reach the nations. And from the start he made that mission a family affair. Abram's name meant "Father," but God changed it to "Father of Nations," or Abraham. His twelve sons would form a great nation that would reach the other nations and bless the entire world—just not alone.

Who Jesus Is

I attended my ten-year high school reunion as a missionary and won the "Most distance traveled" award. But among all the missionaries who ever lived, nobody outdistanced Jesus. He spanned the chasm between heaven and earth on his mission of disciple-making. And at his baptism, the Father and Holy Spirit made it a family affair—even the Son wasn't alone on his mission to make disciples.

Do you know what Jesus's greatest miracle was? At the age of thirty-three, he still had eleven close friends. Bad joke, but good strategy. Before doing anything on mission, Jesus gathered a team around him: allies with him on mission—always sent in pairs, never alone. Jesus modeled for us what it means to walk with others. He grabbed his twos to reach his whos.

Who We Are

The entire New Testament was written *by* missionaries, *to* missionaries, *about* mission. And one of the marks of a mature disciple in Paul's list is being *hospitable* (1 Tim. 3:2). Why? Like Jesus, it begins with spending time, with our allies as well as outsiders. Mission begins with presence, and presence begins with an open calendar, an open home, and a life that's open to others. A missionary can travel across the globe, but if they won't welcome people into their home, they still won't get far.

Think of your two as your support system, which is not a luxury in life but often the lifeline itself. But you can have more than one ally on mission. Paul's allies kept him going. From his deep bond with Timothy, whom Paul called "my true son in the faith" (1 Tim. 1:2), to his affection for Titus, "my true child in a common faith" (Titus 1:4 ESV), Paul's ministry associates were more than companions. They were often the winds in his sails when crossing turbulent waters. David's soul being knit to Jonathan's "strengthened his hand in God" (1 Sam. 23:16 ESV). Elijah had Elisha. Ruth had Naomi. Moses had Aaron and Hur to hold up his arms when they grew too weary. Even Jesus needed friends. Throughout his ministry he walked with the Twelve, but in his darkest hour—in the garden of Gethsemane—he asked his closest friends to stay awake with him. "My soul is overwhelmed with sorrow to the point of death. Stay here and keep watch with me" (Matt. 26:38). At that moment, Jesus needed a friend as he faced his greatest mission.

If the Son of God needed to lean on friends in his hour of need, how much more do we? You have a two to reach your who but take stock of others God has put in your life—your spouse, family, and friends. In time, they'll be a part of your disciple-making journey as well.

FATHER	SON	HOLY SPIRIT
God is a missionary	Jesus was incarnated	We walk with others

Pray This

Father, you didn't design me to be an island. And as much as I may want to be Batman or Batgirl, there will always need to be an Alfred, Commissioner Gordon, and Robin. Make me hospitable not only with my home but also with my time, my words, and my life. Teach me to live in a way that invites others in—through kindness, through presence, and through joy. And as I go about my day, let your mercy flow through me to others. Amen.

Today's Time

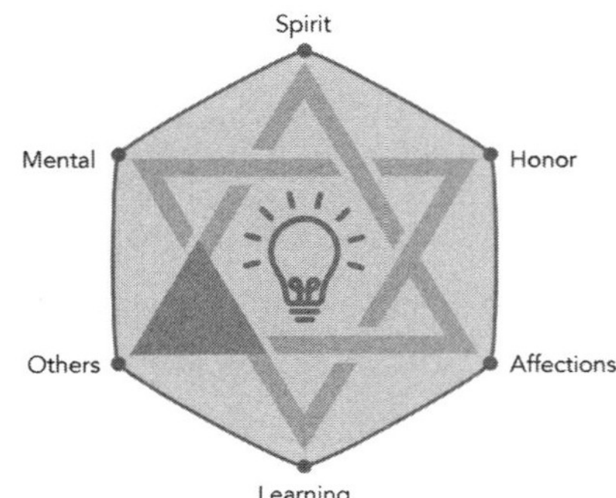

Relationships are key to making disciples. Both those within the community of Christ and those outside of it. So who are your others? The others on mission, and the others who are the mission?

- Share your shalom assessment score with your two.
- What does the relational aspect of mission speak to you about the heart of God?
- Why do you think you scored how you did on the Others part of the shalom star?
- What steps can you take to create more balance going forward?

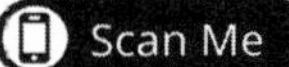

Today's Tactic: Have Fun

In addition to your two, who can you invite to be an ally with you on mission? Someone to pray for you? Someone to check in on you to see how your disciple-making journey is going? Or maybe be your "two" the next time round?

Inviting someone to your home is inviting them into your life. Invite your two and your who over for dinner this week or breakfast on the weekend. Plan a barbeque or something. In other words, have fun.

Big Idea: We walk with others, going with insiders to reach outsiders.

Your Lightbulb Moment

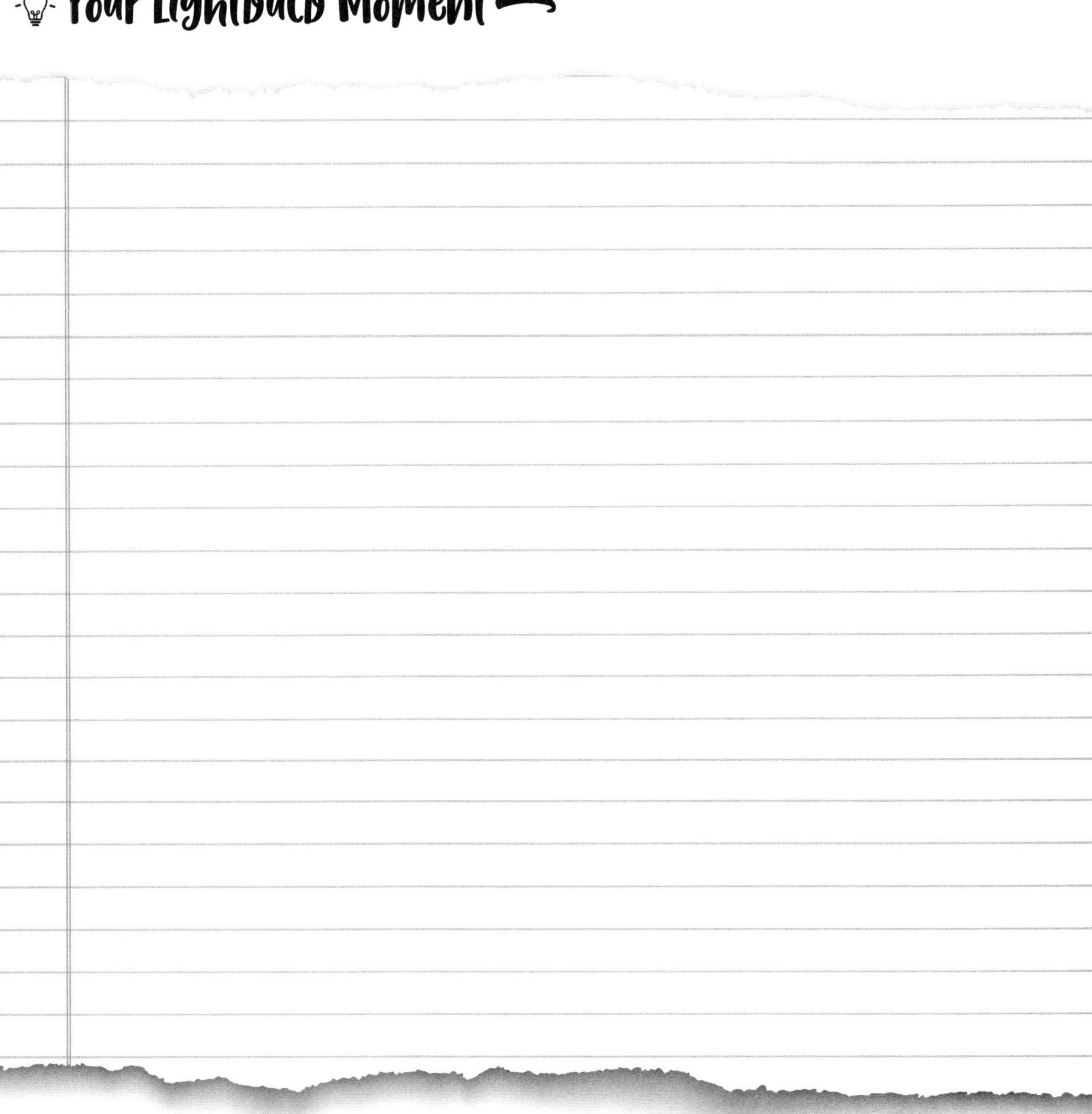

DATE ____ / ____ / ____

STEP 14

Disciples Walk with Mental Toughness

Let us not become weary in doing good, for at the proper time we will reap a harvest if we do not give up.

—GALATIANS 6:9

It's supposed to be hard. If it were easy, everyone would do it.

—JIMMY DUGAN, A LEAGUE OF THEIR OWN

Today's Teaching

Look at you . . . you've made it to the final step in the time rhythm!

So far we've been in the time rhythm, learning the qualities of mature disciples:

They walk in the Light—always transforming.

They walk in the Surrender—living surrendered to God.

They walk in honor—stewarding their God-given responsibilities.

They walk in affection—faithfully loving their families.

They walk in learning—maintaining the posture of a learner.

They walk with others—walking with insiders to reach outsiders.

Finally today, we learn about walking in mental toughness—letting God restore mental wholeness.

Because God allows suffering, mature disciples are mentally tough.

Okay, I'm going to shift gears here. This is sacred ground, so let's tread carefully. As a former psych nurse, I know this section hits close to home for many of you. Before leaving for the mission field, to save up money I left my position as a megachurch pastor to work as a charge nurse in the busiest and most dangerous psychiatric hospital in Southern California. I repeatedly saw people who'd listened to my preaching, now dealing with depression, anxiety, and suicide attempts. I couldn't help feeling that as a pastor, I'd failed so many of them. Back in the 1990s, the church didn't know what to do with mental health. Truth be told, we often still don't. But we're starting to recognize the God-given defense mechanisms he built into us—and how easily they can get bent out of shape.

The Bible may not use the term *mental health*, but it speaks straight to the soul of those who suffer: "The Lord is close to the brokenhearted and saves those who are crushed in spirit" (Ps. 34:18).

Who God Is

If we look at mental health in the Old Testament, Elijah is Exhibit-A. This prophet called down fire from heaven on Mount Carmel, stood against 450 prophets of Baal, and watched God show up in power. And yet, in the very next chapter, 1 Kings 19, Elijah collapsed under a broom tree. One of the greatest prophets in history hit the wall. In modern terms, Elijah had a mental breakdown. Running scared, he begged God to take his life: "I have had enough, Lord . . . take my life" (v. 4). That's debilitating depression in the raw—a crushed spirit, unable to go on.

But notice how God responds. He doesn't scold Elijah, tell him to "just have more faith," or try to exorcise an evil spirit out of him. Instead, he sends an angel with bread and water. Twice. Before giving Elijah a word, God gives him a nap and a meal. Rest and nourishment. God knew that Elijah's body and mind were depleted, and the first step in healing was simple care: sleep, food, and hydration. In today's terms, God treated Elijah's burnout holistically—body, mind, and spirit.

And Elijah isn't alone. Think of Jonah sulking outside Nineveh, asking to die. Or David pouring out his despair in the Psalms: "Why, my soul, are you downcast? Why so disturbed within me?" (Ps. 42:5). The Old Testament doesn't airbrush the mental anguish of its heroes.

What does this tell us? God has always cared for our inner life. Long before modern psychology, the Scriptures show that rest, lament, companionship, and nourishment are part of God's provision for weary souls. Elijah needed more than a pep talk; sometimes the most spiritual thing you can do is rest, receive, and let God meet you in your weakness.

Who Jesus Is

Talking about suffering is a hard conversation, especially for those who've walked through real darkness. Some have endured pain that defies explanation. But Scripture doesn't avoid the topic, but instead walks right into it. Jesus didn't bypass suffering either, but embraced it. His life was marked by hardship—his mental fortitude forged in the quiet struggles of his early years: born under a cloud of scandal and stigma, with whispers about Mary's pregnancy following him into adulthood. As an infant he and his family fled as refugees to Egypt, and he was raised in poverty. After age twelve, Joseph disappears from the story—most scholars believe he died young, leaving Jesus to grow up without an earthly father. Take all these things together, and you see a "man of sorrows, and acquainted with grief" who knew the sting of suffering, and yet was still *deeply* loved by the Father.

Jesus even chose suffering at times - heading straight into the wilderness after his baptism—starving, alone, exposed. There, Satan tested him, questioning his identity: "If you are the Son of God . . ." (Matt. 4:3). In other words, *If God really loves you, why are you suffering?*

That lie still echoes today.

If God loves me, why is life so hard?

Jesus didn't buy it. He knew that suffering isn't a contradiction to God's love, but an accepted part of walking faithfully through a broken world. He would walk that path of pain all the way to Gethsemane, where He prayed, "Father, if you are willing, take this cup from me;

yet not my will, but yours be done" (Luke 22:42). Jesus didn't want to suffer, but he trusted the Father more than his fear.

The truth is, God's love *doesn't* shield us from suffering. But it *does* sustain us in it. "Who shall separate us from the love of Christ? Shall trouble or hardship or persecution or famine or nakedness or danger or sword? . . . No, in all these things we are more than conquerors through him who loved us" (Rom 8:35, 37).

Jesus's life proves, as Job's did, that suffering and God's love for us coexist. Despite being sinless, he suffered terribly in our place. When he cried out, "My God, my God, why have you forsaken me?" (Matt. 27:46), he experienced a depth of abandonment so you never will.

Who We Are

Paul knew this firsthand. His letters repeatedly demonstrate that suffering is one of the ways he grew closer to Jesus. In Philippians 3:10, he writes that he longs to "share in [Christ's] sufferings" (NET). Strange words. But for Paul, suffering wasn't something to run from—it was a doorway to bonding with Jesus, who suffered for us.

Suffering also transforms us. Paul explains in Romans 5:3–5: "We also glory in our sufferings, because we know that suffering produces perseverance; perseverance, character; and character, hope. And hope does not put us to shame, because God's love has been poured out into our hearts through the Holy Spirit." Therefore, our suffering is never wasted, but an opportunity for Christ to carve his character into us. That's how Paul endured beatings, shipwrecks, imprisonment, and mental exhaustion—because he knew it didn't reflect on God's love for him. And in his darkest moments, he discovered that "the peace of God, which transcends all understanding, will guard your hearts and your minds in Christ Jesus" (Phil. 4:7). Only someone wracked by anxiety can write about a peace like that.

William Cowper, best friend of John Newton and his partner in writing "Amazing Grace," struggled with anxiety and depression. Yet few knew of the horrific struggles that beset his life and served as the crucible that forged his words—for Cowper had suffered a mental breakdown at the height of his fame. Considered the greatest poet of his day by Wordsworth, Coleridge, and Jane Austen, many considered his great talents squandered when he quit publishing poetry and focused his talents on glorifying Christ. "God Works in Mysterious Ways" was a poem-turned-hymn penned about how God miraculously intervened in his multiple suicide attempts. In hindsight, he was probably bipolar, but at that time in history that had not yet been understood as a diagnosis. In a day before medication was available, best friend John

Newton would physically hold and restrain Cowper through manic fits of raving and foaming at the mouth when suffering strong delusions and hallucinations. Cradling Cowper in his arms, Newton would pray over him, whispering soothingly to him until it passed. Because the wolf was always at the door, Cowper began to surround himself with things that brought peace and reduced his anxiety. You can visit his house in Olney and stand at the small six foot "summer house" (or as he called it, the "verse manufactory"), where he penned his poems and hymns, nestled in a picturesque English walled garden, surrounded by flowers, bees, and eventually, three pet hares. He took his first hare in when it failed to thrive under the care of a friend's child. Cowper felt that the hare might help aid his mental state, which it did. He wrote, "How cheerful they are in their spirits. How much enjoyment they have of life."[1]

Cowper reminds us that despite our brokenness, God can still use us powerfully. So if your mind and emotions are struggling, hear this: You're not broken. You're human. You're loved. You're not possessed. And you're not alone.[2]

Mental fortitude is not just gritting your teeth and getting through, but surrendering your mind to Christ repeatedly until his peace guards your heart. Our mental state matters to God. And mature disciples know that God allows suffering, as he did with his beloved Son, and we walk with a mental fortitude, knowing we are deeply loved in spite of our pain.

And when that happens, people see a light that isn't from us at all—but Jesus shining through the cracks of our brokenness.

FATHER	**SON**	**HOLY SPIRIT**
God allows suffer-ing as a part of life	Jesus had a difficult childhood	We walk with mental toughness

1. William Cowper, letter to *The Gentleman's Magazine*, June 1784, as reprinted in *Heads and Tales* (transcribed in *The Project Gutenberg eBook of Heads and Tales*), 218.
2. For those struggling, I wholeheartedly recommend *Radically Living, Quietly Dying* by Mike Chong Perkinson, (Light and Life Publishing 2024).

Pray This

God, when pain comes and life doesn't make sense, help me remember that you never leave me or forsake me, just like Jesus promised. Teach me to see your love even in the shadows, to trust that you are good even when our circumstances aren't. Give me the courage to keep going—not because it's easy but because You are with me. Help me not waste my pain, but let it shape me, soften me, and make me more like Jesus. When I am weak, be my strength. When I am lost, be my guide. When I am hurting, be my hope. In the pain of suffering, let me be comforted by your great love. Amen.

Today's Time

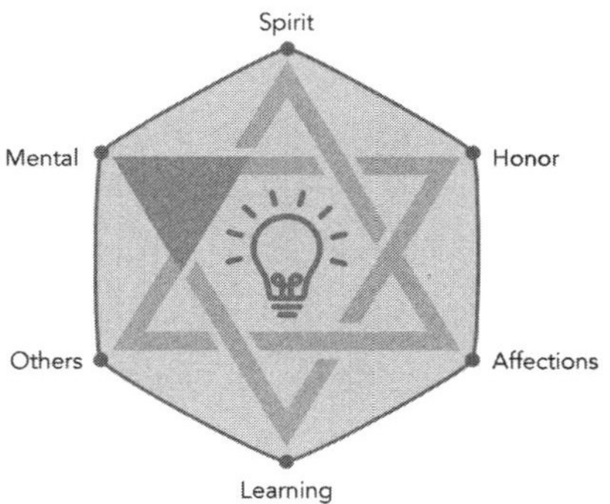

Mental toughness isn't about pretending everything's fine or stuffing down emotions. It's about developing resilience: a steady trust in God that helps you endure setbacks, criticism, grief, and hardship without losing heart. Jesus modeled this perfectly: He acknowledged his grief and cried out in anguish but stayed anchored in the Father's love. The shalom star will help you assess whether you're experiencing the transformation of that kind of resilient mindset.

- Share your shalom assessment score with your two.
- Has suffering tempted you to question God's love for you?
- How does knowing that Jesus suffered as a beloved Son help to shift your perspective?
- Read 2 Corinthians 1:3–7. How do you think God can use your suffering and pain to bring comfort to others?

Today's Tactic: Share What Brings Balance

- Write out one way that you'll obtain shalom balance in your life. That could be getting a good night's sleep, taking a walk, eating well, unplugging from screens, or talking it out.
- Today, take a step to comfort someone who's hurting. First, listen to them and let them know they're not alone. Then pray for them and encourage them.

Big Idea: We walk with mental toughness, knowing that deep pain and deeper love can coexist.

Your Lightbulb Moment

Time
Teaching
Tactics

RHYTHM 2

TEACHING: TRAINING DISCIPLES

Go back in time with me a few thousand years and imagine you're the disciple John. You've been on the road with Jesus this second year, bone-tired at the end of a long day. Sitting around the evening's campfire, under the stars, trying to get warm as firelight flickers across faces still dusty from the road.

Across the flames sits Jesus, debriefing the day with you all. Your blistered feet ache from the journey, but you're still laughing with everyone. Then he looks at each person, his gaze going to you, resting for a second, then moving to the others. And you know in that moment, he's assessing your readiness, what you've learned.

Your mind goes back to the first night you had dinner with Jesus sitting around another fire. You felt back then that Jesus was a secret too good to keep to yourself, and after you left that evening, you had to tell your brother James all about him. *We've found the Messiah.* James looked at you quizzically, perhaps remembering how excited you were about John the Baptist, but something in your tone made him take you seriously. Soon after, James sat around an evening fire with Jesus, getting to know him like you had.

Now, sitting under the stars with Jesus in holy huddles like this, you feel a deep ache: More people should know him this way. There is a weight of sacred guilt—that you've tasted a joy that others haven't.

Years later, you'll pen some of the final words of Scripture with that same ache, inviting others to join you around the campfire with Jesus:

> That which was from the beginning, which we have heard, which we have seen with our eyes, which we looked upon and have touched with our hands . . . we proclaim also to you, so that you too may have fellowship with us; and indeed our fellowship is with the Father and with his Son Jesus Christ. And we are writing these things so that our joy may be complete. (1 John 1:1, 3–4 ESV)

Jesus had done it. He'd reproduced himself in John. He'd made him a fisher of people, willing to leave the warmth of the firelight and push out into the night to catch more people, then bring them back to the fire.

Jesus had made John into a disciple-maker.

Jesus didn't just spend time with his disciples; in his second year, he also trained them. Year 2 was all about preparing them to become disciple-makers.

That's where you are now. In the last seven steps, you and your two walked through the shalom star, focusing on your own transformation - reviewing the marks of a mature disciple. But now it's time to shift gears from transformation to training, from being a disciple to becoming a disciple-maker.

As we enter the teaching rhythm, you'll enter into a training phase. You'll also learn more about the gospel. Jesus kicked off his second year by announcing to the disciples, "I must proclaim the good news of the kingdom of God to the other towns also, because that is why I was sent" (Luke 4:43). Jesus took the disciples out on the road not only to learn the gospel, but to give them a front row seat to what it *does*. It was all preparation for sending them out in the third year to preach it themselves.

But you can't preach what you don't know. If this was the year of teaching, what did Jesus train? What did he want them to learn? Over the next seven steps, we'll focus on what Jesus trained his disciples to prep them to carry on the mission.

Step 15: Learning Grace
Step 16: Learning to Pray
Step 17: Learning to Pursue
Step 18: Learning the Gospel
Step 19: Learning to Share
Step 20: Learning Your Story
Step 21: Learning About Conversations

Entering the teaching rhythm during the second year was a deeper commitment for the disciples. It will be for you too. You're moving beyond focusing on yourself and beginning to observe how the message of Jesus transforms people right where they are. And I can make you the same promise that Jesus made to his six disciples: If you follow him into a deeper commitment, he'll make you a fisher of other people.

DATE ___/___/___

STEP 15

Disciples Learn Grace

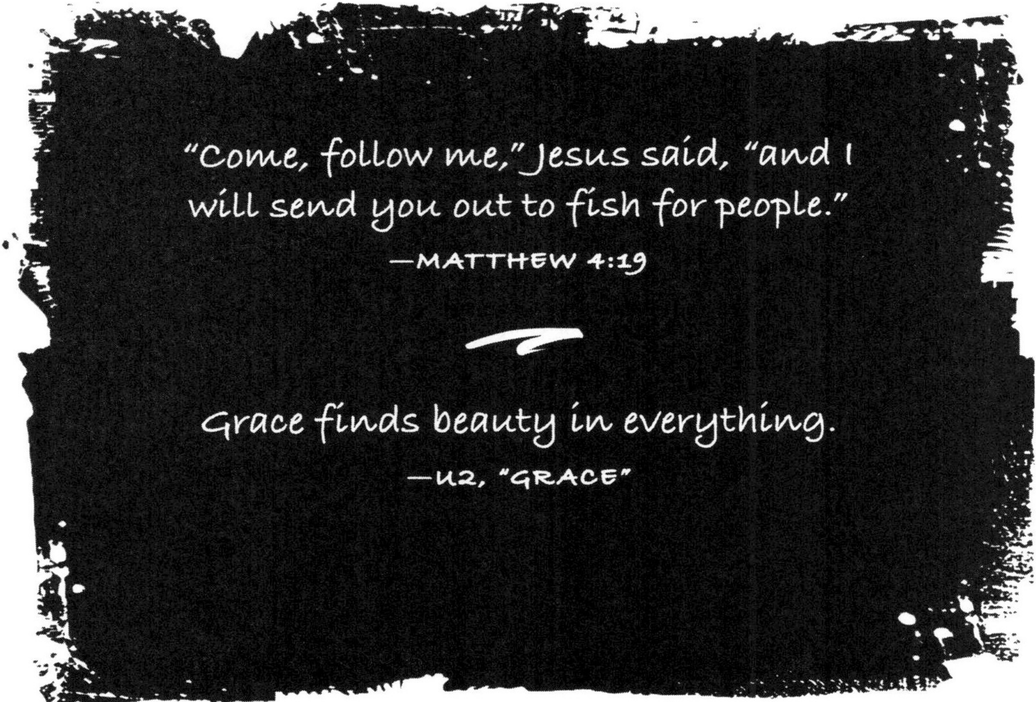

Today's Teaching

Today is our first step in the teaching rhythm. How do you learn best? Some people learn best from audio. Others are visual learners. Still others learn by doing. In the second year, Jesus invited the Twelve into the teaching rhythm where their whole of life was a classroom. Everything Jesus did in that second year was a lesson.

Perhaps the most memorable lesson the original six disciples would learn was when Jesus called his seventh follower.

Matthew could hardly believe his ears.

"Follow me" wasn't what he was used to hearing. More familiar to his ears were the phrases "Why are you following me?" or "Get away from me!"

Having Roman soldiers as drinking companions meant that people left him alone and kept their distance, fearing him as much as they loathed him.

That's why he was so shocked at Jesus's invitation to leave it all behind and follow him. Jesus clearly knew what Matthew did for a living because Jesus called him directly out of his tax collector booth. No conversation, just an invitation.

Matthew knew what kind of man he was, despite his parents' high hopes. They'd named him Levi, after the priests, hoping he might serve God one day. But Matthew loved money, and to secure it, he had to sell out his own people. When the money started pouring in, it felt like he had made the best decision for himself, but now he felt trapped and cheated. Then, Jesus had said, "What does it profit a man if he gains the whole world, but loses his only soul?" Matthew had nearly burst into tears right there.

Matthew had sold out his people, and therefore, sold his soul to the Roman Empire. But something about Jesus's teaching made it sound like anyone could become a part of God's kingdom. Maybe even someone like him. He'd stood at a distance for weeks, listening to Jesus preaching the "good news," feeling that Jesus was staring straight through him. And he'd been in agony since the first time he'd listened.

He'd give it all up if only he could have his soul back. But what he'd done was written in ink as permanent as the records he kept for the Romans. Nobody would ever forgive him . . .

Nobody except Jesus, who'd just said, "Follow me."

It was a no-brainer. A shrewd businessman, Matthew knew an opportunity when he saw it. He immediately left his tax collector booth and followed Jesus, not caring what it would cost him. Matthew knew that second chances, like money, don't grow on trees.

And best of all, Jesus had given him a new name for his new life—Matthew—translated as "grace."

What did it say about Jesus that he called a tax collector as his seventh disciple? He'd promised to make them fishers of people, but they hadn't even left Capernaum yet, and Jesus had just hooked the most notorious sinner they knew.

Jesus was training the disciples about scandalous grace and second chances. During that second year, Jesus taught the disciples what the gospel was as much by his actions as through his words. Every activity, every miracle was an object lesson in grace.

People not looking for God were ambushed by mercy. Demoniacs who'd given themselves to evil spirits were set free. People of all walks of life received miracles before they even knew who Jesus really was. Like Bono sang, "Blessings are not just for the ones who kneel . . . luckily."[1] Through the miracles, people *experienced* grace before they *believed* it.

Do you remember it? The shock when grace first broke into your life? The disbelieving wonder that *you* were following Jesus for real? Don't lose that. Bottle it, because it's lightning. There are still Matthews out there—people just like you who have no idea that grace is coming for them.

And now you get to be the one who brings it.

Your call to others to walk alongside you as you follow Jesus will be just as powerful. The invitation to follow is an invitation of grace. It lets them know that they matter. That they are loved. That grace is real.

As you walk alongside people, they will begin to feel the warmth of grace before they see the light—just like they did with Jesus.

1. U2, "City of Blinding Lights," *How to Dismantle an Atomic Bomb* (Island Records, 2004).

Pray This

Jesus, you were grace in motion. Help me to remember that nobody outside of Christ today is out of the reach of your love. Help me to bring the grace of God into their lives. I thank you for the person who showed your grace to me. Now help me do the same for someone else. Show me who to invest in, when to speak truth, and how to walk with others in love. Make my life a grace-filled invitation for others to follow you. Amen.

Today's Time

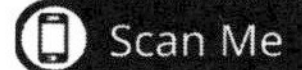

* What does God's grace mean to you?
* Reflect on how grace broke into your life. Who brought it to you? What was your breakthrough moment when you saw the light?
* Who in your life might feel unworthy of grace, like Matthew did? How can you extend Jesus's invitation of love and second chances to them this week?

Today's Tactic: Learning Grace

Okay, final decision time!

* You and your two need to identify your who. You've already been spending time with who potentials in the action steps. Now it's time to narrow it down. Who will you pursue?
* Write their name in the following lightbulb.
* Pray that grace invades their life and breaks into their world. Pray specifically for the Holy Spirit to be working before you even get there.

Big Idea: Grace finds us before we believe—and the same surprise that grabbed you is still waiting out there for someone else.

Your Lightbulb Moment —

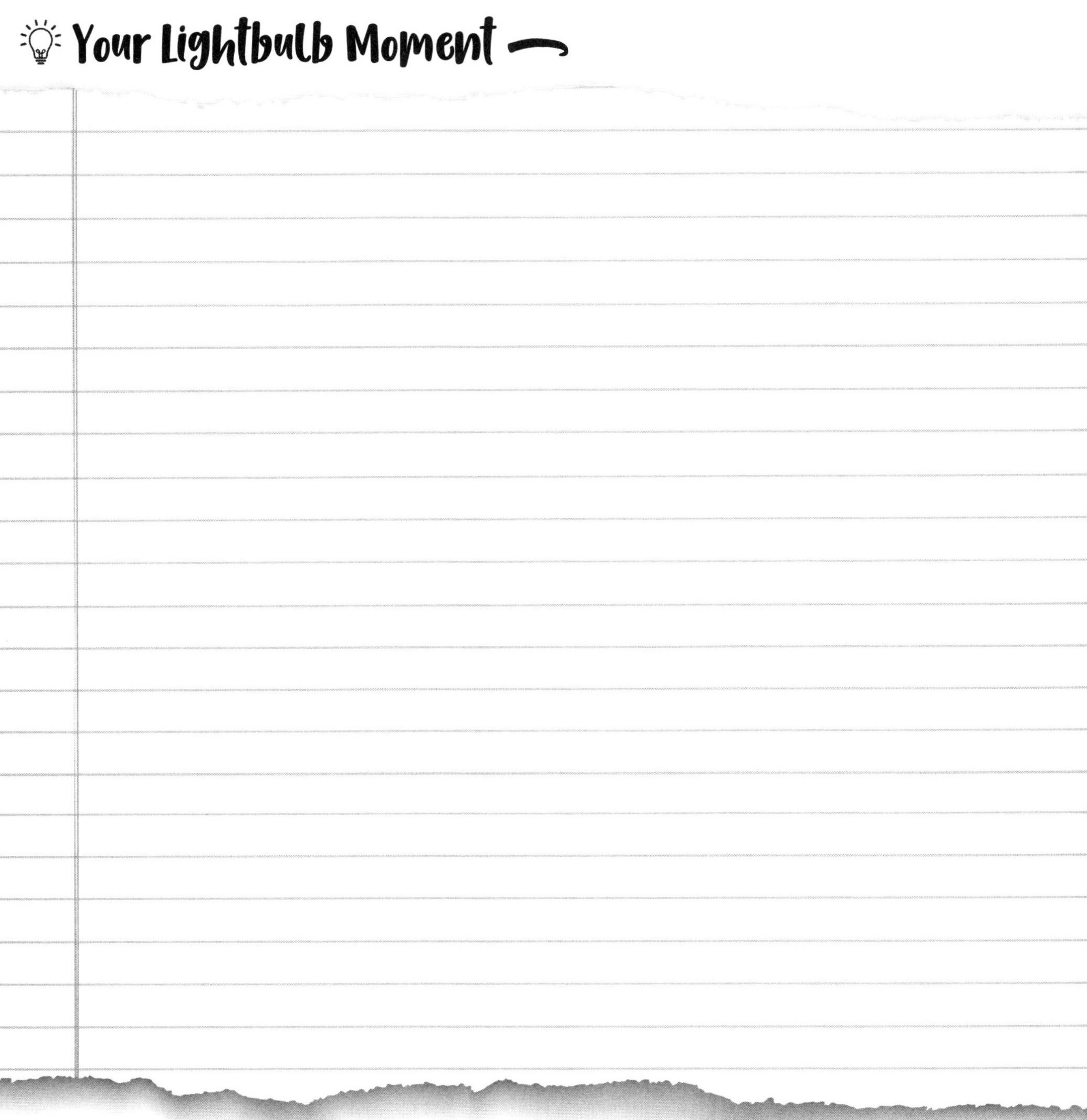

DATE ___ / ___ / ___

STEP 16

Disciples Learn to Pray

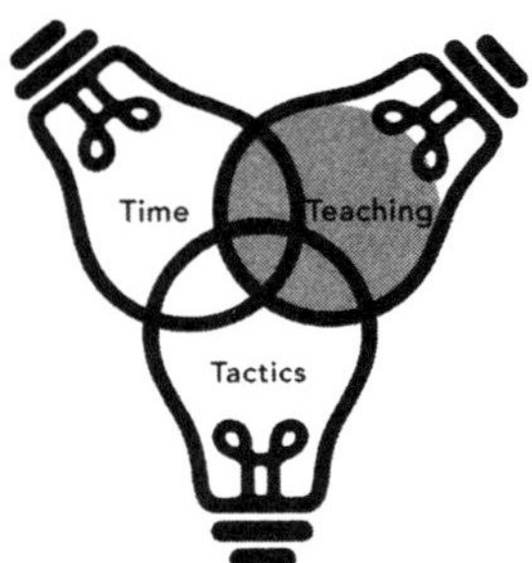

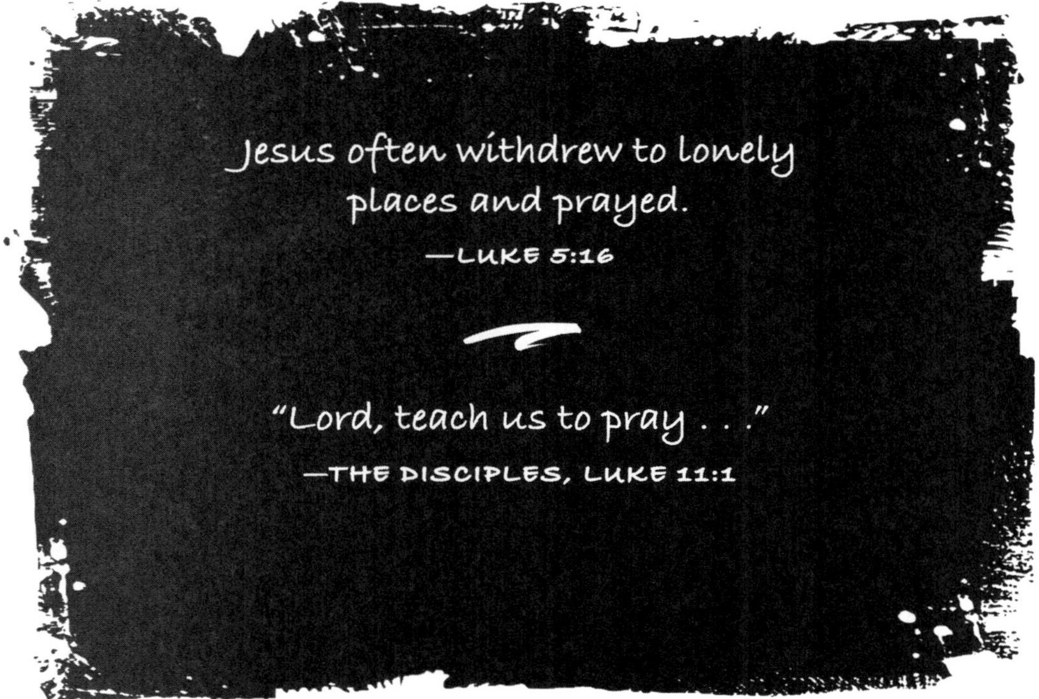

Today's Teaching

Welcome back, disciple-maker. Oh yeah, you got the title now. You're in the teaching rhythm. If you've come this far, you've accepted the second-level invitation of Jesus to become a fisher of people. Big respect, homie and homegirl.

Before we rush out like Samson with our hair cut off, devoid of power and thinking it's all down to our natural ability, let's talk about prayer. Maybe you've struggled to pray. If that's the case, I want you to imagine that you're a believer in the early church speaking with a veteran in the faith. Someone renowned for prayer. Someone who knew Jesus well. You're coming to them for advice about praying.

James the brother of Jesus rubs his chin. "How to pray better?" He laughs softly to himself. "Since I've been given the nickname Camel Knees because of the amount of time I spend in prayer, nobody believes me when I tell them I struggled at the beginning too. But this is why I often sat with James the son of Zebedee, one of the original Twelve disciples, before he was martyred. It was those early days after my brother had risen and appeared to me personally. Many people are shocked to learn that's how I came to believe. I mean, he was just my brother, after all. How I wish I'd believed sooner. There are so many questions I would have asked him."

He shrugs. "I still ask, and sometimes he answers, but prayer isn't really about getting answers . . ." He chuckles again. "I went to James, just like you've come to me. He carried many stories of Jesus like treasures hidden in his heart, and I—hungry as a beggar—would draw them out of him."

James leans back, his eyes drifting somewhere far beyond the room. "One evening, as the lamps flickered in Jerusalem and the sounds of the city grew quiet, I asked him, 'Tell me . . . how did he pray?'"

He looks you right in the eyes and says, "I'll try my best to quote exactly what he said, but my memory isn't what it used to be." He continues, taking on James's voice:

"I remember the first time I noticed it. The fire had burned low and most of us were asleep, but I stirred and realized Jesus wasn't lying there among us. Again. I glanced toward the hills, and there he was, silhouetted against the starlight, lips moving in quiet conversation. It struck me then: He sometimes prayed more than he slept. That's when I began to wonder if this was the source of his strength, the reason he always seemed so grounded, even when the crowds pressed in.

"Later, when he said to us, 'Remain in me, and I in you,' I didn't understand at first. Remain? But the more I watched him slip away to quiet places—sometimes before dawn, sometimes in the dead of night—I realized what he meant. Remaining was prayer. Staying was never leaving that conversation with the Father. There was never a period at the end of his sentences with the Father—there was only a comma.

"Once, I even asked him why he prayed so much. After all, he was the Son of God. Shouldn't the Father already know what he needed? Jesus gave a knowing smile and said, 'The Son can do nothing by himself; he can do only what he sees his Father doing.' I didn't fully grasp it then, but later, when we were gathered in the upper room, I remembered. He hadn't been showing us weakness. He had been showing us dependence. That day, something shifted in me for good. If he needed to abide in prayer, how much more did I?"

James the brother of Jesus sits back. "Well, I have many nicknames now: James the Lesser, James the Just, James the brother of Jesus . . . Camel Knees . . . " He smiles, looking down at his knees, shrugs, and sighs. "I guess the latter speaks to my weakness, to my need and dependency; perhaps that nickname is the biggest compliment after all."

Prayer is a funny thing. It's like evangelism. Prayer and evangelism are two things God never lets us think we're good at. That's because they're both about *dependence on him.*

Both activities place us out of our depth. So it's no surprise that we don't get to be "good at" either one. Evangelism requires his power, and prayer is a confession that we don't have it. When we pray, we take a posture of inadequacy, on our knees, confessing that we need help. And God has linked prayer and evangelism together for that very reason. You see, none of us can save a soul. We can sow. We can water. We can even reap. But God alone makes things grow.

This is why "Jesus often withdrew to lonely places and prayed" (Luke 5:16). Prayer was so central to Jesus's disciple-making that he spent forty days in the wilderness with his Father before calling John and Andrew. During those six weeks, Jesus depended solely on his Father, returning "to Galilee in the power of the Spirit" (Luke 4:14).

If you were a disciple, you observed everything your rabbi did and tried to imitate it. But the disciples really struggled with prayer.

"Where's Jesus?"

"Praying."

"Again? Man, what does he talk about for that long? I run out of things to say after five minutes."

This was what happened when his disciples decided to ask for help. "One day Jesus was praying in a certain place. When he finished, one of his disciples said to him, 'Lord, teach us to pray, just as John taught his disciples'" (Luke 11:1).

We can say we depend on God, but if we don't pray, it's an indicator that we're still trying to handle it on our own. Prayer is the confession of the soul who says, "I don't got this."

So if we want to make disciples like he did, we need to start where he started: *on our knees*. You may not have anything else going in your favor, but with prayer as your starting point, you can move mountains.

Disciple-making machine John Wesley once said, "When I pray, coincidences happen. When I don't, they don't."[1] It's simple. When we pray, God turns up.

Disciple-making always feels like we're the ones late to the party—God, our silent partner—has already been working before we arrive.

Pray This

Father, teach me to pray the way Jesus prayed. Help me to anchor my heart in you before I chase after my plans. Draw me close like a branch to the vine so that your life flows through me. Strip away my self-reliance and replace it with surrender. Remind me that prayer is not wasted time but the work itself. Give me eyes to see people the way you see them. And may every step I take today flow out of time spent with you. Amen.

Today's Time

* How does the time Jesus spent in prayer affect you?
* What difference in your life does it (or would it) make to spend time sitting with the Father?
* What are your biggest barriers to prayer, and what steps can you take to overcome them?

1. Popularly attributed to Wesley, but believed to also have been said by William Temple despite there being no references for it.

Today's Tactic: Establish a Rhythm of Prayer

I'm guessing by now that you've got your who in mind. You've probably been reaching out to them already, but now start taking responsibility for them in prayer. You've already been praying for God to move in the heart of your who wherever they are in Whoville. But now, it's about establishing regular rhythms to pray for them.

- Commit to praying for your who every day.
- Commit to praying for your who every week with your two.
- Practice pausing to pray this week before sending your who a text, or making a phone call. Ensure that prayer always precedes pursuit.

Big Idea: Prayer is where disciple-making starts, because God always gets there first.

Your Lightbulb Moment

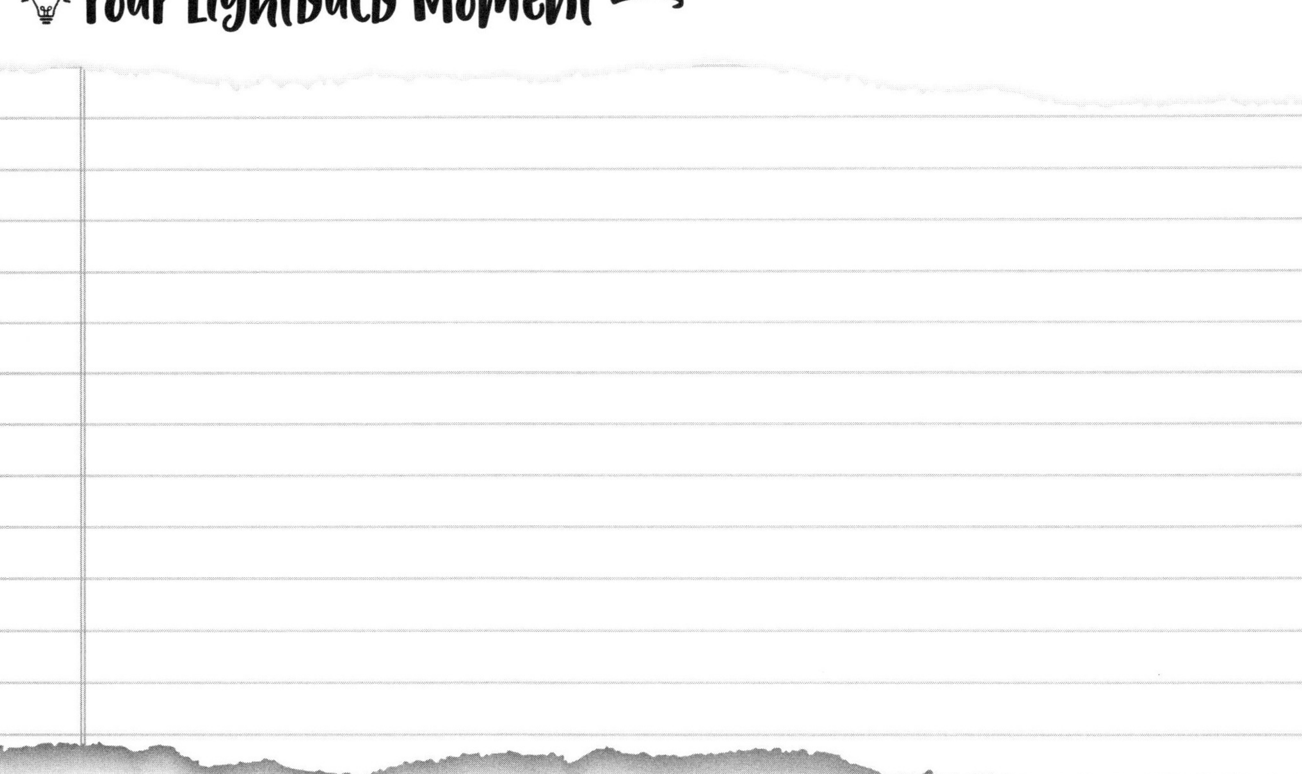

DATE ___ / ___ / ___

STEP 17

Disciples Learn to Pursue

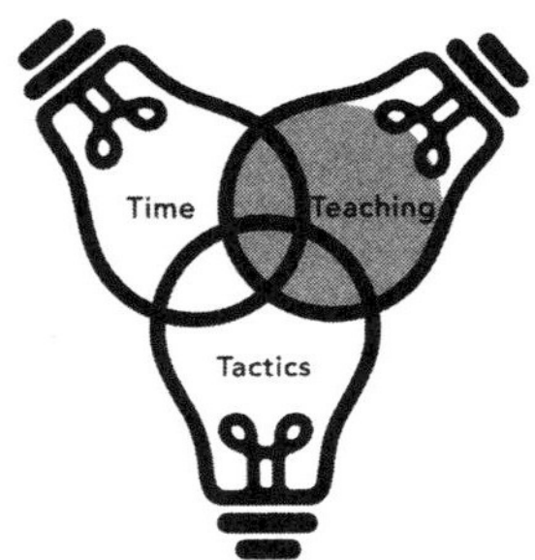

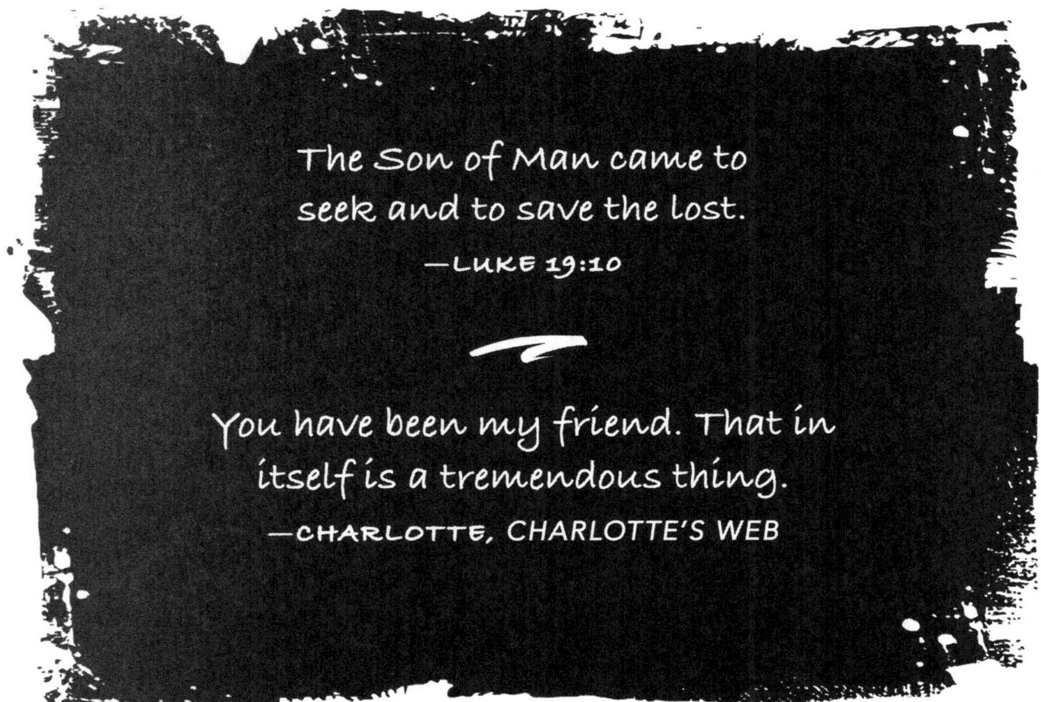

Today's Teaching

Welcome to our third step in the teaching rhythm, where we'll learn about pursuing your who.

> *Zaccheus never thought Jesus would notice him. Too short to see over the crowd, too despised to stand among them. All his life he'd been overlooked. If not passed by, then certainly hated. So he climbed the sycamore tree, hoping to catch a glimpse over the heads of the crowd. Shielded by the leaves, he didn't want Jesus's gaze burning into him. He was a tax collector after all. But then Jesus stopped. He looked up. Right at Zaccheus. Like he knew. Zacchesus's name rolled off Jesus's lips as if he'd always known it: "Zacchaeus, come down immediately. I'm staying at your house today." He couldn't remember the last time somebody said his name without disdain, but Jesus spoke it like a friend. He'd said the unthinkable: they were having lunch as if Jesus had made an appointment. And of course he had. Heaven had long booked this appointment in eternity past.*

So far we've learned that in year 2, Jesus was like a man who came to dispense grace and chew bubble gum, and welp, he was all outta bubble gum. Everyone got grace, like Oprah dispensing cars. "You get grace, and you get grace, and you get grace!" No wonder the Pharisees were so outraged. They were the older brother, jealous that the prodigal sons had come home.

Our first step in the teaching rhythm showed us that disciple-making exists to graciously widen the circle to include those outside of it. Grace finds us before we believe—and the same surprise that grabbed you is still waiting out there for someone else.

Our second step in the Teaching Rhythm taught us that Prayer is where disciple-making starts, because God always gets there first.

And the third step is all about the pursuit. Jesus pursued people. Disciple-makers, like fishermen, pursue their prey. Not like an aggressive salesperson but like a shepherd searching for lost sheep—to seek and save the lost. Those first three steps mean disciple-makers are motivated by grace, bathed in prayer, and in hot pursuit of those who need Jesus.

Years ago, God taught me a lesson about pursuing people. I was a youth pastor, and my youth group was a wreck. Many of them were church kids. They had sat in church all their life, bored. When I preached to the group, they would slump down in their seats, hang their mouths open like they'd fallen asleep, and drool. I found out later they were doing this as a game to pass the time and to try to rattle me.

I was relaxing one Saturday morning when I felt an overwhelming burden from the Lord to go over to one of my youth's houses. The urge felt like, "Go to Nick's house." *Yeah*, I thought, *maybe I will, but man, this cartoon is funny. Maybe later.* But then I felt an alarming urgency: *"Go to Nick's now!"*

I got up, scratching my head because God was talking to me like I was a teenager telling my Mom I'd take the trash out "later." I got up off the couch and switched off the cartoons. "Okay, Lord, I'll go!" I showed up at Nick's house, a first for me. His dad answered the door and said, "Oh, I'm glad you're here. It's an excuse to get his lazy butt out of bed." It was 10:30 a.m.

His dad walked me into the bedroom where Nick dozed, unaware of what was coming. "Hey, Sleeping Beauty, someone is here to see you." Nick's head emerged from under his thick duvet, and in a puzzled voice he mumbled, "Peyton?"

"Yeah, Nick, this is gonna sound weird, but I felt God telling me to come over here. You okay?"

He sat up, wrapped in his duvet so that he resembled a giant creepy, gray grub. He sat there like a larva —equally unresponsive.

"Mind if I sit?"

"Sure."

"Um . . . well . . . I was wondering if I could read the Bible with you?"

He shrugged an acquiescence.

I opened my Bible to 1 John 1:1, the same passage used to disciple me as a new believer. I had used the same method of discipling ever since. It wasn't the best way, I'm sure. It was just what the person who discipled me did.

In that passage, John tells how he was in the inner posse of Jesus and invites us to join his posse too. I asked Nick questions, and Nick nodded, grunted, and mumbled here and there. Then I said, "You know, Jesus wants to be closer to you than you've ever wanted to be close to him. There's no limit to how close you can walk with God, and John is inviting you to know the same love John knew when he called himself 'the one Jesus loved.'" Feeling I wasn't making a dent with Nick, I was shocked when a single tear streamed down his cheek.

That was the moment Nick began to follow Jesus. I left the house stunned, as Nick surrendered his life to the Lord. Bible studies at the youth group and Sunday mornings hadn't done it for him. Nick had sat in my church for fifteen years, never affected by anything that was said, but through one discipleship meeting, Nick had turned on a dime and followed Jesus. Charismatic to the core, Nick was the coolest kid in school, and people soon took notice of his conversion. He became a worship leader in the group and modeled a Christ follower to people in his school. Many kids came to faith because of Nick's witness on campus, and he began to disciple other kids over time. I hadn't known that morning marked a fork in the road for

Nick. I later discovered that Nick and his friends had planned on taking drugs for the very first time that night. Instead, the Holy Spirit derailed those plans that morning with one cartoon-watching knucklehead.

The urgency I felt to visit Nick wasn't imagined. It was very real. Sometimes our hesitation to act and our failure to seize the moment costs us an opportunity to witness to someone.

Nick's story didn't end there. He led others to Christ, discipled his classmates, and eventually married a girl who had once admired his walk with Jesus from afar as an unbeliever. She followed Jesus too—because of him. Nick has since gone home to be with the Lord. But not before taking many others there with him. *It's never a good time to start . . . for us. But it's always a good time to start for others.* So when should you start? *Now.*

The first step, after praying for God to open doors, is to walk through them. If you're an introvert, it can be tough. Funny enough, Nick was one. And nobody ever believes me when I tell them this, but I'm one too. Some people thrive on people juice. Others never touch the stuff. And some must do so in moderation, because how else do you make disciples unless you get around people?

How to tell an introvert how to get around people . . . I know, it's a little weird—a bit like asking someone how to dance. "Move your body," they say. "Just groove to the music," they say. Those people are stupid. Dancing is hard. So is spending time with people.

But if you're an introvert, you're already great at this without realizing it. Because the key to hanging out with anyone is being a good listener. And introverts are natural-born chillers. You make it easy for others to talk.

My disciple-making conversations often sound like an episode of *Friends* (the show about everything) and *Seinfeld* (the show about nothing) all at the same time. A simple conversation over coffee, and soon the person is telling me they fell in love at nineteen, but she broke his heart. Or they can't stop gambling. Or they always carry a knife with them and know it's the scars of the childhood abuse they suffered. Suddenly we're talking about real things now. I listen, I analyze, I ask questions, I ask them to elaborate, and all the while, I'm waiting—waiting for the right opportunity to introduce spiritual truth into the conversation. Because while I'm listening to them, I'm also listening to another conversation—what the Holy Spirit is prompting me to say.

Pray This

Jesus, help me see people the way you saw them—not as interruptions but as treasures worth pursuing. Teach me to seek out the lost, the overlooked, and the hurting, just as you pursued Zacchaeus, the woman at the well, and the one sheep who wandered away. Give me courage to cross barriers, patience to walk with others, and grace to love them into your kingdom. I don't want to pass people by. Make me interruptible, intentional, and relentless in pursuing others with your love. Amen.

Today's Time

- What holds you back from pursuing people? Fear of rejection? Lack of time? Or something else?
- How can you create space for others to share their struggles or stories, and how might you invite the Holy Spirit into those moments?
- When might pursuing your who become too much (like a pushy salesperson)? When is it too little? When is it like Goldilocks—just right?

Today's Tactic: Pursue Your Who

List three things you could do with someone that would feel natural to you. For example, you could go for a walk, play a game, or go surfing. The possibilities are almost endless.

- Pursue your who. Send them a text. Make a phone call. Set up a time to get together and do something with them and your two.
- If possible get together with your who. Don't be discouraged if they don't want to get together again. Keep praying for them, and consider reaching out to your next who if the first one isn't interested in getting together again.
- If you are able to connect with your who, focus on being fully present and listening deeply during your conversation with them. Practice listening and looking for openings.

Big Idea: Following Jesus means pursuing others with the same love that first pursued you. Disciple-makers chase after people, not comfort.

Your Lightbulb Moment

DATE ____/____/____

STEP 18

Disciples Learn the Gospel

He taught as one who had authority, and not as their teachers of the law.

—MATTHEW 7:29

Words are, in my not-so-humble opinion, our most inexhaustible source of magic.

—DUMBLEDORE, HARRY POTTER AND THE DEATHLY HALLOWS

Today's Teaching

This step in our teaching rhythm gets to the heart of it all—the gospel.

If someone asked you to explain the gospel, what would you say? What is the gospel according to you?

The word *gospel* means "good news." Matthew 4:23 tells us Jesus preached "the good news of the kingdom." What was the good news according to Jesus? **The king has come and is bringing his kingdom with him.**

The gospel of the kingdom is not a promise of heaven someday but a declaration that heaven has begun invading earth *now*. And that message came with power. Whenever Jesus preached the forgiveness of sins, he healed, performed miracles, and cast out demons. To be clear, those weren't random acts of niceness. The king was declaring war on sin, death, and hell.

C. S. Lewis captured this beautifully in *The Lion, the Witch and the Wardrobe*. In Narnia, under the Witch's rule, it was always winter—cold, lifeless, and cruel. But when the true king, Aslan, came again, spring invaded winter. His very presence changed the atmosphere—trees budded, and the sun warmed chilled bones as the frozen world thawed in the light of his return. That's what the kingdom of Jesus is like. With the return of the king, all that was lost at the fall of Eden is restored. When the kingdom comes, darkness flees. Paradise lost becomes paradise regained, and with them all the kingdom blessings: The peace of God is restored through peace with God. Our access to him is reopened. Eternal life begins now as our souls awaken. Our purpose is restored. Freedom rises triumphant. And holy desire stirs from its slumber.

Salvation is more than an escape plan. It's the enjoyment of the kingdom blessings restored by the coming of the King.

So how did Jesus restore what was lost?

Unlike most kings who conquer by crushing all resistance, Jesus conquered by surrendering, giving himself to the very ones who defied him. He allowed himself to be arrested, mocked, beaten, and crucified. But that wasn't the worst of it. Hanging nailed to a cross for criminals, suspended between heaven and earth, he bore the full weight of God's judgment.

He died under the wrath of God. Not for His own sin but for mine. For yours.

He lived the righteous life you couldn't live. He died the death you deserved. And in doing so, he satisfied justice and opened the gates of the kingdom for all who would surrender and bow to him.

Because the wrath of God was exhausted on Jesus—completely, finally, forever—there's not a single drop of it left for you or me. Christ's death justified us, meaning God looks at me "just-as-if-I'd never sinned." But you could also say "just-as-if-I'd always obeyed."[1]

That alone should be enough to earn your fealty forever, but Jesus didn't stop at removing your punishment and erasing your debt. By living perfectly and dying innocently, Jesus alone earned our acceptance with God and all the other blessings we lost: peace, access, life, purpose, freedom, and joy. And rising from the dead, Jesus demonstrated that he was the King over everything, including sin, death, and hell. Coming into the kingdom starts with bowing to the king and confessing him as Lord. In short, surrendering to him. It's that simple—despite our attempts to complicate it.

During one mission, a massive crowd pressed in, asking what they had to do to inherit eternal life (John 6:28). Jesus didn't give them a to-do list. He gave them a name: "Believe in the one he has sent" (v. 29).

Just believe. Surprisingly, most of them walked away not interested. Why is believing so hard? Those who asked wanted something they could do. Something they could measure. Something that proved they were worthy. But there will never be something we can point to and say, "*I* did this." We can only point to the cross and resurrection, saying, "He did this."

But we often forget this. That's why believers still need the gospel.[2] Martin Luther is credited as saying, "We need to hear the gospel every day, because we forget it every day." We leak truth like a sieve.

Bob Thune pops the hood on forgetting the cross: When we first come to Christ, the cross is massive.[3] We feel our sin is great and God's holiness is greater, and the cross fills the gap between them. But over time, something shifts. As our behavior improves, we become less aware of our desperate need for forgiveness. As our sin seems more manageable, God's holiness appears smaller. And with it, the cross shrinks. When we forget how sinful we are—and how holy God is—we settle for "little cross" Christianity.

---

1. Jerry Bridges and Bob Bevington, *The Bookends of the Christian Life* (Crossway, 2013), Kindle edition, 26.
2. Peter Jeffery, *Believers Need the Gospel: Reaffirming the Gospel Message for Today's Christians* (Calvary Press, 2007).
3. Robert H. Thune and Will Walker, *The Gospel-Centered Life: Study Guide with Leader's Notes* (New Growth, 2016).

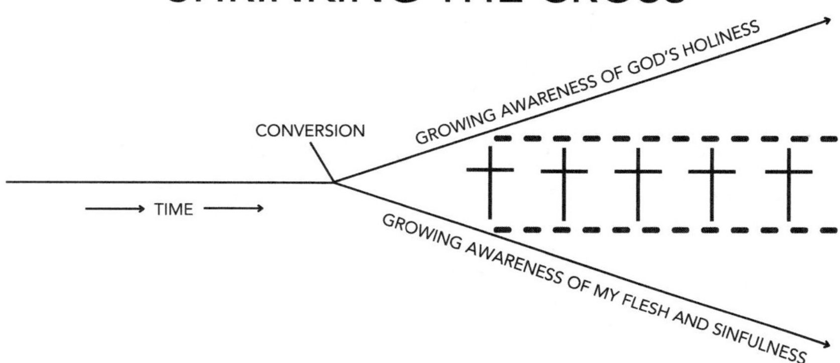

That's when trouble starts.

We minimize or hide our sin. Some become legalists, performing religiously to cover the gap. Others get lax, brushing sin off as no big deal. But at either extreme, we've lost sight of the awesomeness of grace.

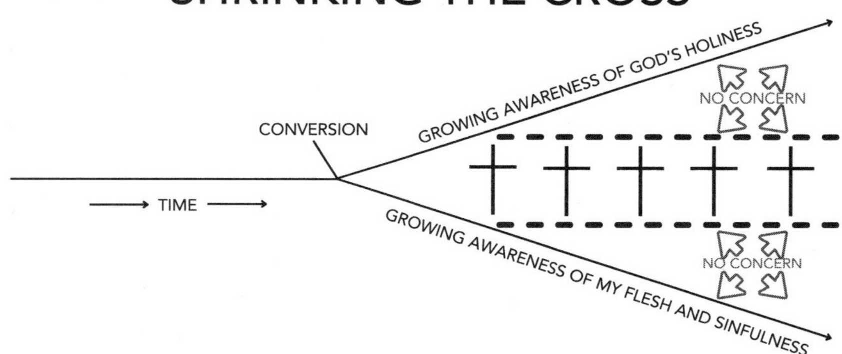

That's why Paul urges, "In view of God's mercy, offer your bodies as a living sacrifice" (Rom. 12:1). Our view of God's mercy matters. Lose sight of it and we drift from the cross. But when we keep God's mercy in full view, our gratitude for grace grows and with it, the cross. If the cross isn't big to us, it won't be big to the disciples we're making. After all, we can't lead others where we haven't gone ourselves—and we should be going to the cross daily.

When we do, the gospel works in us. And "when the gospel works deeply within you, mission is an outcome, not an activity."[4]

4. Mike Chong Perkinson nugget dropped in conversation. We call them MCP nuggets.

THE CROSS CHART

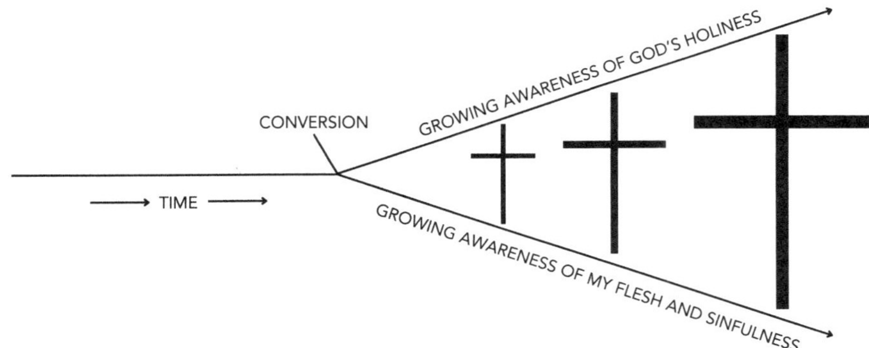

Getting the gospel deep within you is the best way to make sure it comes out of you.

The good news is that in Christ, God's constant desire for you is to experience his grace and peace. His every intention is to draw you near to himself through his Son. That's why in every epistle, no matter what the state of the church, Paul could open with the line "Grace and peace . . ." You may think of it as just a first-century "howdy," but it was an intentional reminder that no matter what state the gospel finds you in at any given time, God desires to pour out his grace on you and restore your *peace*. Otherwise, why would Paul even waste his time writing to some of the churches, as messed up as they were? Grace and peace—that's why! Look over these verses and let grace and peace sink down into your soul.

"Grace to you and peace from God our Father and the Lord Jesus Christ" (Rom. 1:7; 1 Cor. 1:3; 2 Cor. 1:2; Gal. 1:3; Eph. 1:2; Phil. 1:2; 2 Thess. 1:2; Phil. 1:3).

"Grace and peace to you from God our Father" (Col. 1:2).

"Grace and peace to you" (1 Thess. 1:1).

"Grace, mercy and peace from God the Father and Christ Jesus our Lord" (1 Tim. 1:2; 2 Tim. 1:2).

"Grace and peace from God the Father and Christ Jesus our Savior" (Titus 1:4).

"Grace and peace be yours in abundance" (1 Peter 1:2).

"Grace and peace be yours in abundance through the knowledge of God and of Jesus our Lord" (2 Peter 1:2).

"Grace, mercy and peace from God the Father and from Jesus Christ, the Father's Son, will be with us in truth and love" (2 John 1:3).

Pray This

Father, thank you for the gospel—the pure, simple, life-giving news that Jesus has done it all. Forgive me for the ways I add to it, distort it, or drift from it. Teach me to rest in Christ alone, to boast in the cross alone, and to live every moment in full view of your mercy. Help me keep the gospel big in my life—so big that it shapes my heart, my habits, and my mission. When I forget, bring me back. When I waver, steady me. Thank you that grace and peace are not just words but your constant invitation to draw near. I receive them again today. King Jesus, I don't want to put myself at the center of the story. Help me to live in a way that keeps you on the throne—in my heart, my words, my time, and in how I disciple others. I don't want to offer people clever advice or self-help; I want to offer them you. Remind me that the good news isn't about what I've done but what you've done. Make my life a signpost that points to the King and his kingdom. And make me a walking embodiment of his kingdom blessings. Amen.

Today's Time

* How does seeing Jesus as a king—not only a savior—change your view of the gospel?
* If someone asked you, "What is the gospel?" how would you answer?
* Who in your life needs to experience grace and peace from you right now in tangible ways?

Today's Tactic: Spreading Grace and Peace

* Today, go out of your way to show someone the grace and peace of God by doing something that helps them experience it.
* In the conversation that follows your actions of grace and peace, tell somebody about the grace and peace the kingdom brings.

Big Idea: Conversations can carry the message of Jesus, so start speaking and listening.

Your Lightbulb Moment —

DATE ___ / ___ / ___

STEP 19

Disciples Learn to Share

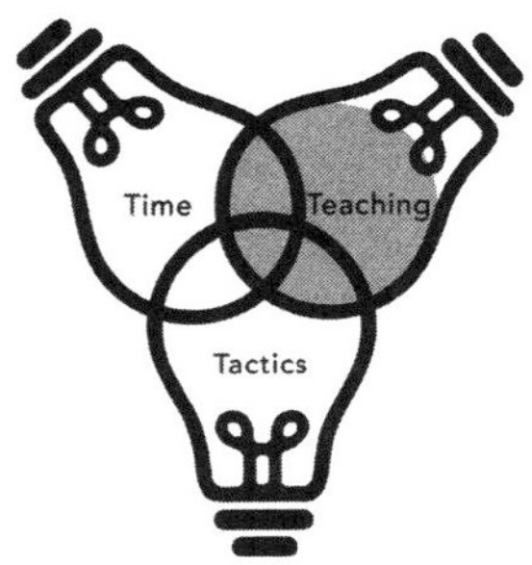

Let your conversation be always full of grace, seasoned with salt, so that you may know how to answer everyone.

—COLOSSIANS 4:6

If you just communicate, you can get by. But if you communicate skillfully, you can work miracles.

—JIM ROHN

Today's Teaching

Now that you know what the gospel is, how do you communicate it?

That's what this step is all about. The disciples listened to Jesus's conversations about the gospel. They heard him talk to people about their souls. And sure, it helped. But just like you and me, they sometimes still found themselves struggling for the right words to say.

If you've ever wondered how to return to talking about Jesus when the conversation keeps going back to Bigfoot or aliens, you're not alone. Conversations about spiritual things can spiral in the strangest directions. One minute you're tracking with Jesus, the next minute you're in Area 51. Welcome to the front lines, soldier! Take courage, the Holy Spirit is still at work, even in the weird tangents.

One of the biggest challenges disciple-makers face is that we're not all speaking the same language. You might be talking about grace or sin or salvation, but the person across from you has no idea what those words mean. They've heard them, sure. But they've never *understood* them. They know the vocab but not the definitions.

That's why Jesus spoke in pictures and told stories. He used metaphors drawn from everyday life, speaking on topics they understood to explain what he knew they didn't. Even with a respected religious teacher, Jesus used a picture: "You must be born again."

Nicodemus was stunned. "Wait—what? How can someone be born twice?"

Exactly.

That was the point. Jesus used something Nicodemus *already understood*—birth—to explain something he couldn't yet grasp—new birth by the Spirit. And suddenly, Nicodemus realized that Jesus was talking about doing something miraculous inside him, something he'd never experienced before, something completely new.

Jesus didn't adjust truth to fit the listener, but he *did* change how he communicated it depending on who was in front of him. He spoke to fishermen about casting nets, to farmers about sowing seed, and to shepherds about lost sheep. Jesus shared the gospel in a way that *made sense*, something every disciple-maker needs to work at.

One of my favorite examples of someone using a metaphor to communicate the gospel is from Bono, the lead singer of U2. For years, the rock star has been open about his faith in Christ. When interviewed for his book *Bono on Bono*, he was asked why he was a Christian. Here's how Bono responded:

> You see, at the center of all religions is the idea of Karma. You know, what you put out comes back to you: an eye for an eye, a tooth for a tooth, or in physics; in physical laws; every action is met by an equal or an opposite one. It's clear to me that Karma is at the very heart of the universe. I'm absolutely sure of it. And yet, along comes this idea called Grace to upend all that "as you reap, so you will sow" stuff. Grace defies reason and logic. Love interrupts, if you like, the consequences of your actions, which in my case is very good news indeed, because I've done a lot of stupid stuff . . . But I'd be in big trouble if Karma was going to finally be my judge. I'd be in deep muck. It doesn't excuse my mistakes, but I'm holding out for Grace. I'm holding out that Jesus took my sins onto the Cross, because I know who I am, and I hope I don't have to depend on my own religiosity . . . But I love the idea of the Sacrificial Lamb. I love the idea that God says: *Look, you cretins, there are certain results to the way we are, to selfishness, and there's mortality as part of your very sinful nature, and, let's face it, you're not living a very good life, are you? There are consequences to actions.* The point of the death of Christ is that Christ took on the sins of the world, so that what we put out did not come back to us, and that our sinful nature does not reap the obvious death. That's the point. It should keep us humbled. It's not our own good works that get us through the gates of heaven.[1]

Do you see what he did? He changed the vocab to karma, knowing that most people believe in it. Changing the vocab isn't changing the truth. Behind Bono's use of karma was the biblical truth of judgment—and against that, grace looks beautiful. He didn't change the gospel itself; he just communicated it in language the interviewer and millions of readers could understand. As an apologist, C. S. Lewis did the same thing with the Eastern concept of the *Tao* to describe objective truth and moral order.[2]

Remember, at the end of everything, disciple-making is mission work. You're taking the light into darkness, and in the darkness there's not much illumination. So when you bring the bright light of the gospel somewhere, you might sometimes have to let people's eyes adjust.

So if someone wants to talk about Bigfoot or aliens, roll with it! First, ask them what they think. And if you give an answer, bring it back to Jesus. You can say something like:

---

1. *Bono on Bono: In Conversation with Michka Assayas* (Riverhead, 2005), ch. 11.
2. C. S. Lewis, *The Abolition of Man* (1943).

What do I think of aliens? That's a great question. C. S. Lewis—who wrote *The Chronicles of Narnia*—wrote a sci-fi series where he imagines that life on other planets might exist—planets that never rebelled against God like ours did. In his second book, *Perelandra*, he imagines a kind of "second Eden" and shows how God could still be true and good and present, even if there were intelligent life out there.

God made the whole universe. And just like he relates to people differently in different cultures, he could relate to other beings too, without contradicting who he is. The Bible says that Jesus created *all things*, including things in the heavens we haven't even discovered yet.

So if aliens existed, it wouldn't disprove God. It would mean his creativity is even more vast than we thought. And his love would still be big enough to reach them too.

Practice makes perfect, and the more you practice these types of conversations, the better you'll get at them. And believe me when I say, you'll even start to have fun. After all, who doesn't love to talk about Bigfoot and aliens?

Pray This—

Jesus, you never seemed thrown off when people asked strange questions. You met each person where they were and spoke in ways they could understand. Teach me to do the same. Give me patience when the conversation drifts and wisdom to steer it gently back to you. Help me see people not as projects but as stories you're already at work in. Let my words be clear, my tone be kind, and my heart be full of grace. Thank you that the power is not in my eloquence but in your Spirit. Amen.

Today's Time—

- Have you had a conversation about faith that went sideways—aliens, Bigfoot, conspiracy theories, or something else? How did you respond?
- What are some common spiritual-but-not-religious ideas you hear in your circles (for example, universalism, atheism, crystals and chakras, ghosts)? How could you use one of those ideas as a bridge to explain the gospel without watering it down?

Today's Tactic: Share the Gospel with a Character

You know how I said that disciple-making can be fun?

Pick a fictional character you know well. It could be from a movie, book, show, or comic. Then imagine they ask you, "So, what's the deal with Jesus?"

Your job is to explain the gospel in a way that *they* would understand—not with churchy language but in terms that speak to their world, values, or wounds.

Step 1: Choose a Character

Here are a few to get you started, but feel free to introduce your own:

* **Darth Vader** (*Star Wars*)—The coolest ever! Conflicted and shaped by regret
* **Elsa** (*Frozen*)—Isolated and afraid of hurting the people around her
* **Katniss Everdeen** (*The Hunger Games*)—Cynical but with a strong sense of justice
* **Joy** (*Inside Out*)—Always keeps a happy face on but struggles deep inside with identity
* **Pick your own**

Step 2: Map Their "Spiritual Profile"

If you get stuck, ask yourself the following questions:

* What do they care about most?
* What lies have they believed about themselves?
* What would they find hard to believe about grace?
* What words or metaphors would confuse them—or connect with them?

Step 3: Now Write It

Write two to four sentences that explain the gospel in a way this character would understand. You're not dumbing it down—you're speaking their language.

Example

To Darth Vader:

You thought power could save you, but it only enslaved you. Grace is different—it doesn't control or dominate. Jesus doesn't force you to the light. He calls you out of the dark because he already faced it for you.

I know, that went over some of your heads. As an aside, let me say that a firm grasp on pop culture is an excellent tool in the disciple-maker's tool kit. The important thing is that you learn to start applying the gospel to the stories of the people around you.

Big Idea: Even after understanding the gospel ourselves, communicating it in a way that makes sense to others is our next challenge.

Your Lightbulb Moment

DATE ___ / ___ / ___

STEP 20

Disciples Learn Their Story

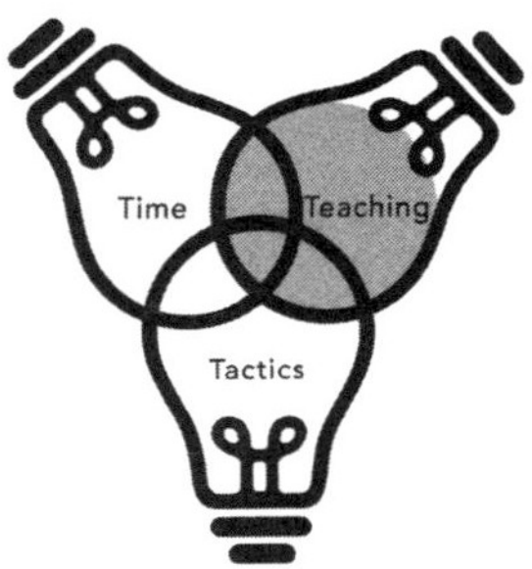

Many of the Samaritans from that town believed in him because of the woman's testimony, "He told me everything I ever did."

—JOHN 4:39

The most powerful person in the world is the storyteller.

—STEVE JOBS

Today's Teaching

The Bible doesn't hand us a cookie-cutter script for sharing the gospel. Instead, the New Testament gives us a raw, messy mix of real conversations. And one of the most powerful tools you have as a disciple-maker is your own story of meeting Jesus.

So far in this journal, we've retold some of the stories of disciples straight from the Gospels. The gospel writers knew the power of story, and so should we. The gospel isn't just *the* gospel. When you tell your story, it also becomes the gospel *according to you.*

So what's your story?

In a world where people question everything, they may argue against your beliefs, poke holes in your reasoning, or disagree with your worldview, but they can't easily argue with *your story.* They can debate a doctrine, but how do you dismiss an encounter? In a culture that bows to relativism, experience has the last word—and nothing speaks louder than a head-on collision with Jesus.

If anyone is proof of that, it's Paul. In Acts, the Holy Spirit gave us not one but *three full tellings* of Paul's story (Acts 9, 22, and 26). In ancient times, writing materials like papyrus were pricey. But telling the story three times was well worth the cost because a well-told story in the Spirit's hands can pierce bulletproof hearts faster than any argument ever could.

Though Paul was a master of logic and Scripture, he didn't lead with an academic lecture. He led with *what happened to him.* How in the past he would have killed for what he would die for today; going from a violent persecutor to a devoted follower of Jesus. And each time he told it, the shape of the story flexed just slightly, not because the truth changed but because his audience had. That's called gospel agility—the ability to hold tightly to the truth while speaking it in a way that connects to the heart of the person in front of you.

Paul wasn't the only one to use this strategy. C. S. Lewis did the same thing in *Surprised by Joy,* his own story of coming to faith. Lewis had been an apologist, debating with atheists for years, but in the end, he found story to be the most compelling way to present Jesus, just like the Gospels. He simply told the story of how God chased him down until Lewis finally gave in and called himself "the most reluctant convert in all England."[1]

It was the first step on Lewis's personal Damascus road.

And you've had your own version of an encounter with Jesus on that road. Your story matters as much as anybody's. You don't have to have a dramatic "rock bottom" testimony, serve

---

1. C. S. Lewis, *Surprised by Joy: The Shape of My Early Life* (New York: Harcourt, Brace, 1956), 236.

jail time, or survive some headline-worthy ordeal. God can still use you to light the path for someone else—because sometimes the quiet stories are the most relatable.

Let's look closer at Paul's three tellings and how they can help us share our own stories today. In Acts 9 we get the original report of Paul's conversion, told by Luke. It reads like a documentary: Paul's on the road, gets blinded, hears Jesus speak, and ends up in Damascus, where he's healed and baptized. It's factual, vivid, and direct.

This version is all about *what happened.*

This is the best approach with someone who's skeptical or analytical: "This is what I was like. This is what happened. This is how I changed." Think ESPN highlight reel—"Here's the score as it was, here's the moment everything turned, here's the win." The real evidence is your transformed life—the light you shine—that backs up your story like evidence.

Then in the second example, Acts 22, Paul speaks to a crowd of religious Jews in Jerusalem and gives them more details about his religious upbringing: a student of Gamaliel, zealous for the law, passionate for the traditions of the ancestors. Then he pivots: "I persecuted the followers of the Way . . . until I saw the light." Paul switches it up in a way that resonates with *them.* His emphasis is on how his whole life was shaped by zeal and how Jesus redirected that zeal into true worship. They could relate because they felt that same zeal but also shared his struggle to please God. In this case, Paul isn't pointing to the light radiating from his life, he's pointing them to the source of its power!

If your testimony mirrors the life of someone who's spiritual, religious, or trying to be a "good person," you can meet them where they are. You can tell them you've tried that route and that Jesus didn't make you *better*; he made you *new.*

Finally, in Acts 26, Paul is standing in front of King Agrippa and the Roman governor Festus. These aren't religious fanatics this time—they're educated, political, skeptical. Agrippa is a backslidden Jew. Festus, a pagan. So Paul leans into the fulfillment of prophecy. Festus thinks him crazy. Agrippa thinks him persuasive. But both leave with a sense of fear and an ominous sense of being on the wrong side of the judgment of God. Sometimes when people didn't accept Jesus as Savior, Paul left them with Jesus as Judge.

In each case, Paul used the same core story, yet with gospel agility he adapted the way he told it depending on the person listening. Paul knew the power of the gospel. "I am not ashamed of the gospel, because it is the power of God that brings salvation to everyone who believes." (Rom. 1:16). And the gospel often travels fastest through your story, because when people hear how Jesus has changed you, they start to wonder what he could do for them.

So here's the challenge. Can you write out your story in three ways?

- One that simply tells the facts: *what happened, what changed.*
- One that relates with someone's experience who doesn't know Jesus.
- One that speaks to someone who isn't religious at all—who simply wants meaning, peace, or purpose.

Share and adapt your story because this world is full of people like Nicodemus who know the vocabulary but don't understand the definitions. It's also full of people like Agrippa and Festus who are curious but scared to release the hold of the throne on their own lives. And it's full of people just like you once were, waiting for someone to tell them a simple story that gives them hope.

Pray This

Jesus, thank you for giving me a story worth telling. You didn't only change my circumstances—you also changed my heart. Help me remember that my story is really about you: your grace, your power, your love. Give me courage to share it, not with pride or performance but with honesty and hope. Show me how to speak in a way that connects with the person in front of me. Make my story a window for someone else to see you clearly. Use my past, my present, and even my pain to point people to your goodness. Amen.

Today's Time

- If someone asked you, "Why do you follow Jesus?" how would you answer in three minutes or less?
- What are some moments in your life when you clearly saw God at work before you were a Christian?
- Who in your life might need to hear the "facts" version of your story? Who might need the "meaning" version?

Today's Tactic: Listen to Your Story

* Record one-, two-, and three-minute voice memo responses to someone asking you, "Why do you follow Jesus?" Use your real voice. Don't script it. Speak from the heart. Then replay it. What sounded clear? What felt confusing or vague? What would you change next time?
* For extra credit, share your testimony with someone this week. To set it up, ask them what they think the meaning of life is, and let them speak first. After that, share your testimony in three minutes or less.

Big Idea: Your story matters because it points people to Jesus.

Your Lightbulb Moment

DATE ____ / ____ / ____

STEP 21

Disciples Learn About Conversations

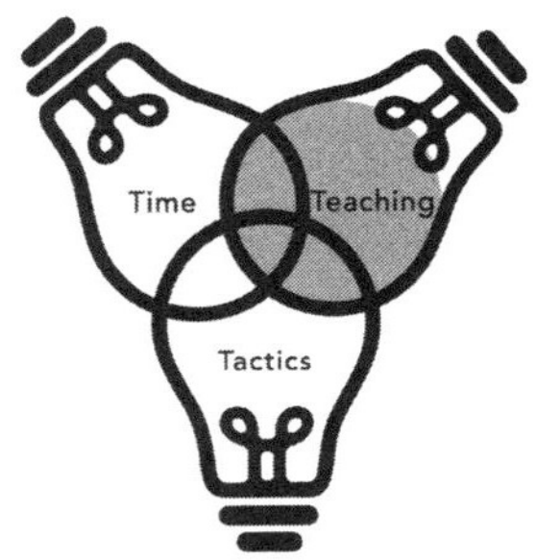

Always be prepared to give an answer to everyone who asks you to give the reason for the hope that you have. But do this with gentleness and respect.

—1 PETER 3:15

What you do in life echoes in eternity.

—MAXIMUS, GLADIATOR

Today's Teaching

Words hold unimaginable power. For every word in Hitler's seven-hundred-page *Mein kampf*, five hundred people died. Words can destroy—but words can also redeem. That's why John introduces Jesus as *the Word made flesh*. John's gospel is built on conversations—one-on-one encounters. It holds more red-letter real estate than any other gospel, and it's 77 percent dialogue.

If I were to subtitle John's gospel, I'd call it *Conversations with Jesus*.

Do you know why it's considered the most evangelistic book in the Bible? Because *conversations lead to conversions*. John says it plainly: "These are written that you may believe" (John 20:31).

John exclusively highlights conversations such as the following:

- Nicodemus in the dead of night
- The Samaritan woman at the well
- The man born blind
- Mary Magdalene at the empty tomb
- Pilate in the governor's palace

These stories are meant to help us see ourselves in each of these people. Nicodemus, confused and searching for answers. The woman at the well, hiding shame. The man born blind, unjustly hurt by religious people yet "seeing" something different in Jesus.

One of the most famous sentences ever recorded was from a conversation with a religious teacher named Nicodemus, who opened with, "Rabbi, we know that you are a teacher who has come from God." (John 3:2). He came under the cover of night, afraid to be seen with Jesus in public. Rather than mocking Nic-at-Night for sneaking in the shadows, Jesus listened—and then dropped the most quoted line in history: "For God so loved the world . . ." (John 3:16). That single late-night exchange has led millions to Christ over the last two thousand years.

That's the power of words. The power of a single conversation.

We may never know the full ripple effect of a single dialogue with one person. Big doors swing on small hinges, and your small conversation might swing the door of salvation wide open for someone.

Take Edward Kimball. Hardly anyone knows his name, but one trembling visit to a shoe shop changed eternity. As a young salesman knelt to fit him for shoes, Kimball told him about Jesus. That salesman was Dwight L. Moody, who went on to become one of the greatest evangelists of the nineteenth century. Millions of lives swung on that small hinge. And yet almost nobody remembers the man who opened the door. Like Edward Kimball, you may never be famous either, but you might be one conversation away from changing the world.

No pressure, right?

So why am I telling you all of this? We're on the last step of the teaching rhythm, and I want you and your two reaching out to your who to become a lifestyle rather than an event. I want the training wheels to come off the bike eventually and for you to learn to ride without holding the handlebars.

That's what Peter wanted for the people he was discipling: "Always be prepared to give an answer to everyone who asks you to give the reason for the hope that you have. But do this with gentleness and respect" (1 Peter 3:15).

When you find that conversations lead to conversions, you look for opportunities to have more of them. I don't want to give you the impression that you always need to have "the *big* conversation." You know, the sales pitch. Even sharing your own personal story about how you came to Jesus is like Daffy Duck on Vaudeville drinking the exploding potion: "I can only do this trick once."[1]

So let me put a new tool in your tool kit that will help crack open more conversations for you. In the last step we talked about telling your story, but have you ever heard of a microstory? It's a short testimonial about something God is doing in your everyday life.

Imagine walking into work Monday morning, where people are talking about what they did over the weekend. And you say something like, "Man, I was in a major pickle over the weekend, but God really came through once I handed everything over to him."

Nothing major. Just a microstory that opens the door a crack for someone. If they don't tap on the door, you move on, but eventually microstories spark a conversation. The people you're discipling may start sharing microstories of their own, saying things like, "I was at the golf course the other day, looking out over the green as the sun was coming up, and I realized how blessed I am. I'm not religious, but for the first time in my life I thought I should say thank you to somebody up there."

Remember, Jesus promised he'd make his disciples fishers of people. As experienced fishermen, they knew that patience is one of the greatest qualities of fishing. Getting people hooked usually happens through a series of ongoing conversations rather than one high-pressure sales call.

---

1. Daffy Duck, *Show Biz Bugs*, directed by Friz Freleng (Warner Brothers, 1957).

As we've explored in the teaching rhythm, making disciples isn't about perfection or a single method—it's about showing up, engaging in meaningful conversations, and trusting the process. There are many right ways to make a disciple, but the only wrong way is not to do it at all.

Pray This

Jesus, I don't want to make disciples of me. I want to make disciples of you. Teach me to walk with people the way you walked with yours, with grace, patience, honesty, and love. Help me to never lose sight of the fact that this is about relationship, not results. Make me someone worth following, only because I'm following you. Thank you for never giving up on me. Help me do the same for someone else. Make me someone who doesn't only talk about disciple-making but truly lives it. Use my life, my story, and my scars to bring someone closer to you. I'm ready to show up. Just show me who to walk with. Amen.

Today's Time

- Why do you think conversations are so important in disciple-making?
- What small opportunities do you have to share a microstory about God's work in your life? How can you make sharing these stories a natural part of your everyday conversations?
- Consider the people in your life. Who might be searching for hope, like Nicodemus, or carrying shame, like the woman at the well? How can you approach them naturally with gentleness and respect to share the reason for your hope?

Today's Tactic: Share a Microstory

- Share a microstory this week with your who, or anyone else, and see how it goes.
- Pat yourself on the back for completing your Jedi training in disciple-making. And take the next step into the tactics rhythm—see you there!

Big Idea: Life-changing encounters often begin with simple words. Your conversations carry eternal weight.

Your Lightbulb Moment

Time
Teaching
Tactics

RHYTHM 3

TACTICS: SENDING DISCIPLES

Congratulations. You've now made it to the tactics rhythm.

This is where everything changes.

There's a scene in *The Lord of the Rings: The Fellowship of the Ring* where Samwise Gamgee pauses, closes his eyes, and lifts one foot up, hovering mid step. Frodo turns around and says, "Sam, what are you doing?"

"Mr. Frodo, if I take one more step, it'll be the farthest from home I've ever been."[1]

We've spent time learning how Jesus transformed his disciples in year 1 through the time rhythm and how he trained them in year 2 in the teaching rhythm. Now we step into the third and final year of his earthly ministry—the year of tactics. This was the season when Jesus moved his disciples from simply learning to doing, when Jesus flipped the switch and sent them out. He activated them. Imagine that morning when they all woke up to receive more training, and he surprised them with an announcement. Let's join them as they tried to process what he told them at the dawn of year 3 as they entered into the tactics rhythm.

1. *The Lord of the Rings: The Fellowship of the Ring*, directed by Peter Jackson (New Line Cinema, 2001).

They'd been following him for nearly a year now, listening, watching, soaking it all in. He healed diseases they didn't even have names for, and spoke with the authority no rabbi dared to claim. Everywhere they went, the crowds pressed in. Sometimes it felt like they were just along for the ride, spectators in the front row of the greatest show on earth.

Then one morning he called them together - the air heavy, like something was about to change. His eyes scanned their faces—ordinary fishermen, a tax collector, a zealot, brothers, friends. And then he said it: They were going out on mission.

Out? Us? Without him?

They half-expected him to laugh, to say he was joking. But he commenced delivering instructions like a commander briefing his soldiers: "Go to the lost sheep of Israel. Proclaim that the kingdom of heaven has come near. Heal the sick. Raise the dead. Cleanse lepers. Drive out demons."

They looked at each other, wide-eyed, bewildered expressions, mouths open. Stunned. Was this some kind of joke? Did he just say raise the dead? Then stomachs churned as reality set in. He was handing them his authority, like a master craftsman passing the tools to apprentices who'd barely learned how to hold them.

And yet there was something steady in his tone. He told them not to pack a bag, not to carry money, not even an extra shirt. Just go. Trust God. Trust the people God had already prepared to welcome them. "The worker is worth his keep," he said.

Jesus began putting them into pairs. Some waited around to ask questions; others shuffled off, conversing in hushed whispers, comparing notes in their confusion. They couldn't explain it, but as terrifying as it sounded, some of them felt a strange courage rising within their chests. If he believed they could do it, maybe—just maybe—they could.

That day, the lines blurred. They weren't just watchers anymore. They were being sent.

That third year was bookended by mission trips—first the sending of the Twelve and later the sending of the Seventy-Two. Between those two trips, the disciples got all their hands-on experience. They passed out bread and fish that multiplied in their fingers. They prayed for the sick and saw them recover. Peter even took a few trembling steps on water. And on the mountain, they glimpsed Jesus in his unveiled glory.

That's where you are now in this journey. You've been training the last seven steps, but now the next seven steps will initiate you into the tactical rhythm. Think of them as practice missions. Nothing overwhelming, just small stretches to get your feet wet, to give you the feel of what it means to make disciples in real time. After all, Jesus didn't hand his disciples the whole world on day one; he gave them short-term assignments that built confidence and dependence on him. And he'll do the same with you.

Rather than flinging them out into the unknown, Jesus provided them with essential instructions. You can find them in Matthew 10, and we'll be applying their principles to your practice.

And don't worry about not feeling ready. The truth is, you'll never feel completely ready for the mission of disciple-making. None of Jesus's disciples did. But Jesus knew that the only way to learn disciple-making was to release them to do it. Aristotle nailed it when he said, "For the things we have to learn before we can do them, we learn by doing them."[2] This is known as the tactile learning style, and it's highly effective.

So from here, you'll learn by taking action—fumbling at times, failing forward, and discovering along the way that Jesus truly does go with you. These next seven steps are designed to help you practice, stretch, and begin to live out what you've been training for.

So are you ready? Take a deep breath, take the hand of your two, and let's step into the tactics rhythm together.

This is where the adventure begins.

---

2. Aristotle, Nicomachean Ethics, trans. W. D. Ross (Chicago: Encyclopaedia Britannica, 1952), II.1, 1103a32.

DATE ___ / ___ / ___

STEP 22

Disciples Are Sent as Witnesses

These twelve Jesus sent out with the following instructions: "Do not go among the Gentiles or enter any town of the Samaritans. Go rather to the lost sheep of Israel."

—MATTHEW 10:5–6

No, no! The adventures first. . . . Explanations take such a dreadful time.

—LEWIS CARROLL, *ALICE'S ADVENTURES IN WONDERLAND*

Today's Teaching

The disciple-making strategy of Jesus was not a matter of "Wait and see who shows up," but "*Go and make disciples.*"

Right after saying that, Jesus's last words to the disciples before being taken up to heaven were, "You will receive power when the Holy Spirit has come upon you, and you will be my witnesses in Jerusalem and in all Judea and Samaria, and to the end of the earth" (Acts 1:8 ESV).

I used to think "the ends of the earth" meant some remote jungle. A mountain village with no Wi-Fi or running water. A place that needed passports, immunizations, and maybe a machete.

But one day it hit me: I'm already there. To the disciples Jesus said those words to, I'm on the other side of the world, a continent away—at the ends of the earth!

Wherever you're reading this from L.A. to Lima, Sydney to Singapore, you're living proof that the gospel made it all the way there. Jerusalem was the epicenter, and the gospel spread from Jerusalem, to Judea, to Samaria, and finally to the ends of the earth. That means you're the fulfillment of Jesus's words in Acts 1:8.

But now it's your turn. Jesus didn't say to be missionaries or to be evangelists, because most of us would paint ourselves out of that picture right away.

He said to be his witnesses.

I can be a witness, right? And you can too, right? I mean, all that a witness needs is to have seen or experienced something they can testify about. I've experienced Jesus. My eyes have been opened to him as the Lord of all—and I can testify to that. I may not be the best witness, whatever that means, but it's my experience. Jesus wants me to tell people what I've seen and heard. That's all the disciples did after seeing the risen Lord Jesus. When the authorities told them to stop, they answered, "We cannot help speaking about what we have seen and heard" (Acts 4:20).

How can I not tell what I've seen or heard of Jesus? How can you not?

Since most of us find ourselves *witnesses* at the ends of the earth, we shine Jesus wherever we are right now. The office. The neighborhood. The laundromat. And yes, even online.

You don't need a plane ticket to obey the Great Commission. You just need to live sent where you are right now.

Live sent?

That's right, because if you're already on the mission field, God wants to use you right where you are. Living sent is a posture. It means that wherever you go you're on mission. So whether you're in Jerusalem, Judea, Samaria, or scrolling on your phone at Starbucks, you are already on the mission field. The question isn't *if* you're sent but *how* you'll live now that you know you are.

To get them ready to live sent, Jesus sent the Twelve on a short-term mission trip, "Do not go among the Gentiles or enter any town of the Samaritans. Go rather to the lost sheep of Israel" (Matt. 10:5–6). First, he told them not to fling themselves far and wide but to reach the people in their own neighborhood. That means living sent starts with the people around you. Second, he called them lost sheep. That means the Good Shepherd is looking for them. You were once the lost sheep. Don't forget how far the Shepherd went to bring you home—and how far he's willing to send you for someone else.

Pray This

Lord, thank you for those who went, who gave, who prayed, who shared—until someone brought me the good news. Now I want to carry it forward. Show me how to be your witness, here and to the ends of the earth. Open my eyes to whom I can reach, send, or support. Help me to live sent wherever I am . . . at least until you send me somewhere else. Thanks for the opportunity to "go" in your name. Amen.

Today's Time

* How does the idea of being a witness, rather than a missionary or evangelist, change the way you think about sharing your faith? What have you seen or experienced about Jesus that you can testify to?
* What kind of witness do you think you've been so far? What do the people around you think about Jesus because of you?
* How might your life change if you lived "sent" to your own neighborhood?

Today's Tactic: Invite Your Who

Okay, time to live sent.

* This week, reach out to your "who" again and invite them to spend some time together. It might be your second or third time meeting, and that's good—you're building trust. Don't overthink the activity; what matters is the relationship. Share something you enjoy—coffee, a walk, hitting golf balls, a Pilates class, even tinkering on a car. The point isn't the activity itself but showing genuine interest in them and creating space for real conversation.
* Make sure that you do the next step before getting together with them. Think of the next two steps as a combo move!

Big Idea: You are God's witness, sent precisely to where you are.

Your Lightbulb Moment

DATE ___ / ___ / ___

STEP 23

Disciples Are Sent with the Word

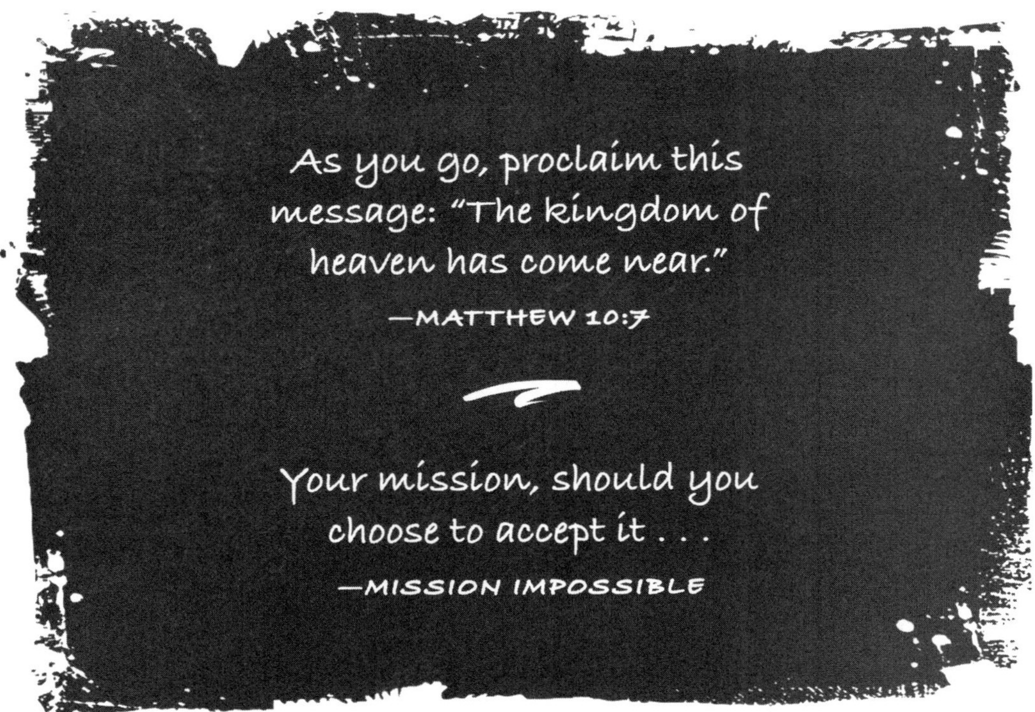

Today's Teaching

MI6 would never dream of sending James Bond out on a mission without Q first equipping him with the right gadgets, weapons, and gear. In the same way, Jesus never sends us out empty-handed—not flashy gadgets, but with God's Word. "As you go, proclaim this message, 'The Kingdom of heaven has come near'" (Matt. 10:7).

Join me out in the desert with Philip, armed only with the word, as he witnesses the private kingdom of a diplomat get invaded by the King of Kings.

> *It wasn't the kind of place you'd expect a divine appointment. Just a dusty road winding south from Jerusalem to Gaza. The kind of sunbaked stretch where travelers kept their heads covered and their water safe. You didn't come to this place unless you had to—and then you passed through it as quickly as possible. And yet that's exactly where the angel of the Lord directed Philip to go. The Spirit told Philip, "Go to that chariot and stay near it" (Acts 8:29). No detailed briefing, no map marked with an X; just a simple instruction to go and a road that stretched into the unknown like a question mark.*
>
> *Philip had just come from the revival fire in Samaria, where the Holy Spirit ripped through people like a wind: diseases evaporating, demons fleeing, baptisms causing a splash. From the flurry of activity, Philip was pulled away without warning and sent into the quiet, empty desert.*
>
> *And then, through the shimmering heat of the road ahead, he saw a chariot kicking up a dust cloud on its way to intercept him. Not just any chariot but a royal one. Inside sat a man of status and significance: a high-ranking Ethiopian official, the royal treasurer returning home from court business in Jerusalem. In his hand, was the scroll of Isaiah, as his eyes scanned the ancient words, heart straining to understand. And in an instant Philip realized why he was sent.*

To be clear, this wasn't Philip the apostle. And that's important. This was Philip the deacon, chosen by the apostles in Jerusalem. Not one of the original Twelve, Philip didn't have a front-row seat to Jesus's ministry. Like us, he missed the calming of the storm and the multiplying of the loaves. Philip was a second-generation disciple. That's why he's the perfect case study for us. He's not the blueprint but the build. Like us, he was forced to rely on handed-down principles from Matthew 10. And this passage shows how he mastered them.

Trendy methods change with fads, but principles can be adapted to multiple situations.

And out in the desert in Acts 8, Philip needed them. He was out of his depth and found himself blazing a disciple-making trail nobody could map out for him. It was just Philip, the Ethiopian, and the Spirit—out in the middle of nowhere.

"The eunuch asked Philip, 'Tell me, please, who is the prophet talking about, himself or someone else?'"

My football coach used to talk about the linemen widening a gap so big you could drive a Mack truck through it. Once Philip saw the opportunity yawn wide before him, he launched it like Evel Knievel over Snake River Canyon.

"Philip began with that very passage of Scripture and told him the good news about Jesus" (Acts 8:34–35).

It doesn't get any easier than that.

There's a reason Philip started with Scripture. When you're helping someone discover Jesus, Scripture is the most powerful way to let God speak. "For the word of God is living and active, sharper than any two-edged sword, piercing to the division of soul and of spirit, of joints and of marrow, and discerning the thoughts and intentions of the heart" (Heb. 4:12 ESV). Last time I checked, I lacked the power to do any of that. But I have the same Scriptures that Philip had. From the very pages of Isaiah, God declares,

> So shall My word be that goes forth from My mouth;
> It shall not return to Me void,
> But it shall accomplish what I please,
> And it shall prosper in the thing for which I sent it. (Isaiah 55:11 NKJV)

In other words, the Word never misses the mark; it always hits its target. Even when it seems like nothing is happening, God is planting seeds, preparing something eternal. Walking alongside someone through Scripture has been working for me for thirty-five years, and engaging Scripture means Jesus isn't just speaking through me, he's speaking for himself.

In Acts 8, Philip modeled a crash course in disciple-making 101, engaging all three rhythms: time, teaching, and tactics.

- Tactics: He was sent on mission and went.
- Time: He sat alongside someone who was spiritually curious and went on a journey.
- Teaching: He opened the Scriptures and led him straight to Jesus.

Now fast-forward to today. How do we repeat this without supernatural teleportation or royal chariots? Simple: Reach into your pocket. That rectangular distraction machine we call a phone might be the most powerful disciple-making tool you own. And why not? Jesus always used whatever was already in the field—loaves, fish, fig trees, even a borrowed donkey. If he were sending you out today, he might paraphrase his commands to the Twelve: *Don't pack anything extra—just take your phone.*

And here's why using the Word matters—most people aren't as closed off to it as you might think. Eighty-five percent of people say they want to understand the Bible better, but the two obstacles are these:

1. They don't have a lot of time.
2. When they try to read the Bible, they can't understand it.

They don't need a preacher; they need a Philip—someone who will come alongside them at their convenience and ride shotgun with them as they discover Jesus. That's where the Discipology plan on the Through the Word app comes in. It mirrors Philip's encounter in Acts 8, giving you a chance to stay close to someone and walk through the Word with them.

Specifically, you and your two will take your who through the gospel of John. It includes ten-minute audio guides that you can listen to daily or weekly. Right there in the app, you'll be able to text or leave audio for one another in a private group. It's like sitting in the chariot with someone, only now you're both holding phones instead of scrolls. It's relational, practical, and completely free.

Over the years, I've always incorporated the Bible into my disciple-making. It doesn't matter which social activity we're engaged in—at some point while we're hanging out, conversation will lead to God, and it will be an excuse to crack open the Bible later and work through something. I'll play Lieutenant Columbo, asking them what the passage means. I'll have them wrestle through it. Then we'll talk, pull out principles, pray together, and call it a day. But after I've closed my Bible, their hearts remain open, and his Word continues to speak.

But with the Discipology Plan, it's all laid out for you. You and your two will tell them that you're going to be starting a regular exploration of John's gospel for people who don't understand it. You'll invite them to walk alongside you as you explore who Jesus was. No chariot required.

Pray This

Lord, thank you for giving us your living Word. Just as you sent Philip to the Ethiopian, send me where you want me to go. Give me courage to come alongside others with patience, listening ears, and a heart that points them to Jesus. Remind me that your Word has power to change lives even when I feel weak. Amen.

Today's Time

* What do you notice about the way Philip begins with Scripture and points directly to Jesus?
* Who in your life might be spiritually curious, like the Ethiopian official, and how can you come alongside them to explore Scripture together?
* What tools or resources, such as your phone or a Bible app, can you use to make disciple-making more accessible and practical in your daily life?

Today's Tactic: Ride Shotgun with Scripture

* Between you and your two, decide which of you will start a new John plan on Through the Word. Once one of you has opened a new plan, invite the other into it. This is the plan you will invite your who into when they agree to study John's gospel with you.
* Ask your who if they would be open to reading the gospel of John with you. To make it easy, you can invite them to the Through the Word plan, which takes ten minutes per chapter. There, you'll be able to interact with your who the same way you've been interacting with your two.

Big Idea: God's Word does the heavy lifting, so trust it to open the lid on people's hearts.

Your Lightbulb Moment —

DATE ____ / ____ / ____

STEP 24

Disciples Are Sent with Expectation

Heal the sick, raise the dead, cleanse those who have leprosy, drive out demons. Freely you have received; freely give.

—MATTHEW 10:8

If you do not expect the unexpected, you will not recognize it when it arrives.

—HERACLITUS

Today's Teaching

Step 3 in the tactics rhythm . . . so how's it going?

One of my favorite things when running our Discipology cohorts is to hear the stories at this stage in the game. And if you haven't already, you're going to start having stories of how God turned up . . . just like Nathanael did.

> *"I saw you while you were still under the fig tree."*
>
> *Nathanael froze. He hadn't told anyone about that moment.*
>
> *It wasn't only because Jesus had seen him physically; it felt like this stranger had looked into Nathanael's soul. That fig tree, Nathanael's hiding place, was his quiet place of prayer and pondering. That's how Philip knew he'd find Nathanael in its shade, heart heavy, wrestling like Jacob with questions about how to be blessed by God.*
>
> *Jacob, the grandson of Abraham, may have been one of the "fathers of Israel," but he wasn't a saint. Jacob's second name, "Israel," still clung to the nation like a second skin. But story beneath the name—that was the stuff of scandal. Jacob lying for his birthright, deceiving his father, supplanting his brother. Nathanael had grown up on those stories, but lately they haunted him. If there was hope for Jacob, maybe there's hope for me? Jacob was so full of guile and cunning, and though Nathanael felt far from guileless, he wracked his brain trying to understand why Jacob still received favor from God. Nathanael didn't understand it then, but it wouldn't be long before the word grace would explain everything. There Nathanael sat, wrestling with the gap between who he was and who he longed to be. He knew he needed a Jacob-style collision with God—maybe then he'd find the answers—but sitting there, he had no earthly idea how to find him.*
>
> *Right then Philip came running, breathless: "We've found the one Moses wrote about . . . Jesus of Nazareth!" Nazareth? Nathanael's skepticism flared. "Can anything good come out of Nazareth?" It was a throwaway line to shield himself from disappointment in another would-be messiah.*[1] *But Philip was so insistent that Nathanael slowly got up and followed him back to wherever he'd met this so-called-Messiah.*

---

1. A. B. Bruce speculates that "Nathanael's prejudice against Nazareth sprung not from pride, as in the case of the people of Judea who despised the Galileans in general, but from humility. He was a Galilean himself, and as much an object of Jewish contempt as were the Nazarenes. His inward thought was, 'Surely the Messiah can never come from among a poor despised people such as we are-from Nazareth or any other Galilean town or village!'" A. B. Bruce, *The Training of the Twelve: How Jesus Christ Found and Taught the 12 Apostles* (New York: George H. Doran Company, 1917), 33.

Philip's face had never looked so full of hope, so Nathanael followed him to a ring of young people circling a man around thirtyish. Jesus fixed on him with knowing eyes as he approached and said, "Here truly is an Israelite in whom there is no deceit."

Those few words sliced through Nathanael's doubt like a blade. No deceit. No guile. It wasn't a description. It was more of a declaration. But Jesus didn't see only who Nathanael was; he saw who he could be. In a flash, he realized: This man didn't simply know him; he saw the Jacob in him and called him Israel—what God was making Jacob into; a man with no need for guile. Jesus was speaking into a moment so private, wrestlings and heartache so deeply personal; it was a moment that only God could have known about.

"How do you know me?"

Jesus answered, "I saw you while you were still under the fig tree before Philip called you."

Nathanael's skepticism collapsed instantly. "Rabbi," he said, "you are the Son of God; you are the king of Israel."

Nathanael moved from thinking about Jacob's story to living it—he'd encountered God—and, like Jacob, was being offered a new identity.

"You believe because I told you I saw you under the fig tree? You will see greater things than that. Very truly I tell you, you will see heaven open, and the angels of God ascending and descending on the Son of Man."

Jesus tells Nathanael to be expectant. "You will see greater things than that" is another way of saying, "Oh, you think that's a big deal? You ain't seen nothing yet." And it's true. Nathanael hadn't.

You probably haven't either. I don't say that to insult you, but it wasn't until I was engaged in the tactical rhythm that I began to see healings, exorcisms, and the supernatural taking place. They aren't commonplace, and they weren't in Acts either, but they still happened. And they still do.

They will for you too, like it or not. When you go on God's mission, he just turns up. In the Great Commission, Jesus promised his presence and power would be with those who go. So don't be surprised when he actually does it. Like I've always told people I train, the more front-line you go, the more like Acts it gets.

That's what Jesus wanted them to know when sending out the Twelve: "Heal the sick, raise the dead, cleanse those who have leprosy, drive out demons. Freely you have received; freely give" (Matt. 10:8).

That must have been almost as scary as the "Don't take an extra bag, tunic, or money" part. But Jesus wanted them expectant that God would turn up. And when they returned from their trip? They were talking excitedly about all God had done. "Demons listened to us . . . to us!" and "People were healed" (see Luke 10:17).

It can be funny for us to read how shocked they were and have the attitude of "Yeah . . . um . . . duh! Jesus kinda told you to do that stuff. You shoulda expected the Holy Spirit to turn up." Except that's us too. He's also told us to expect him to turn up on our disciple-making journey, and yet we're often still caught between being scared because we don't think he will but are blown away when he actually does.

Stupid is as stupid does, and we're pretty stupid for a while as disciple-makers. Thank God he turns up for stupid and smart alike.

Pray This

Lord Jesus, you see me even when I feel hidden. Thank you for knowing not just who I am but who I can become. Help me to expect you to show up in ordinary conversations and unexpected places. Give me eyes to see others the way you see them and faith to believe you are already at work before I arrive. Amen.

Today's Time

* In the story of Nathanael, how does it strike you that God promised to surprise him with even more amazing demonstrations of the Holy Spirit?
* Where in your life do you need to expect God to "show up"—to see you, know you, and speak into your story?
* Who is one person you can approach with expectancy this week, believing Jesus is already at work in their life?

Today's Tactic: Walk in Expectancy

In an earlier step, you established a habit of praying for your who before calling or texting. Now your action step is to establish the habit of praying for yourself before going into a meeting, phone call, or coffee. Pray for the Spirit's power and presence as promised in the Great Commission, "I will be with you." Pause and pray, "Jesus, I expect you to already be here. Help me notice what You're doing." Then look for signs of his presence.

Big Idea: When we go, we expect the Spirit to show up and empower us.

Your Lightbulb Moment

DATE ___ / ___ / ___

STEP 25

Disciples Are Sent with Dependence

Do not get any gold or silver or copper to take with you in your belts—no bag for the journey or extra shirt or sandals or a staff, for the worker is worth his keep.

—MATTHEW 10:9–10

The gift of God is the Holy Spirit.

—SAINT AUGUSTINE

Today's Teaching

Congrats for making it to tactics step 4. If this were a popular language app, you'd be racking up a solid streak by now, unlocking a little cartoon disciple-making owl. But this is about more than building streaks or badges. It's about building dependence on God.

Jesus knew what he was doing when he sent out the Twelve with nothing extra. No bag. No spare tunic. No emergency fund stuffed in the money belt. Why? Because he wasn't only teaching them to preach the message of the kingdom, he was also teaching them to *depend on the King*. It wasn't about traveling light. He was training them in dependence. He stripped away their backup plans and disoriented them on purpose so they'd have to rely on him. No backup plan. No safety net. Just faith that God would provide.

Unnerving, isn't it? To walk into a mission stripped down, vulnerable, and a little uncomfortable. But that's how we learn that disciple-making doesn't run on our self-sufficiency. It runs on trust.

That's why Jesus had to fling them out of the nest like a disciple-making mama bird. It was the only way to get them to depend upon God for themselves. Maybe that's how you're feeling today—still scared. Advancing in haltering footsteps, obediently, but with shaking hands and trembling legs.

You're not the only one who still gets scared. The grizzled veteran of disciple-making, the apostle Paul got nervous. Don't believe me? He *repeatedly* asked for prayer for boldness: "Pray also for me, that whenever I speak, words may be given me so that I will fearlessly make known the mystery of the gospel" (Eph. 6:19).

Paul admitted fear, weakness, and total dependence on the Spirit. But check this out. That dependence on the Holy Spirit led to power. "And I was with you in weakness and in fear and much trembling, and my speech and my message were not in plausible words of wisdom, but in demonstration of the Spirit and of power." (1 Cor. 2:3–4 ESV).

And it wasn't just one time. Paul felt the same pressure to stay quiet and play it safe, so he asked for prayer that he wouldn't shrink back:

In Ephesians 6:19–20, he asks, "Pray also for me . . . that I may declare it fearlessly, as I should."

In Colossians 4:3–4, he pleads, "Pray for us, too, that God may open a door for our message. . . . Pray that I may proclaim it clearly, as I should."

In 2 Thessalonians 3:1–2, he says, "Pray for us that the message of the Lord may spread rapidly and be honored. . . . And pray that we may be delivered from wicked and evil people."

In Romans 15:30–31, he writes, "Join me in my struggle by praying to God for me . . . that I may be kept safe from the unbelievers in Judea and that the contribution I take to Jerusalem may be favorably received."

Can you hear the dependence in Paul's requests for prayer? And it wasn't just Paul. Even the Twelve were daunted at times and gathered to pray for boldness in Acts 4:29–31: "'Now, Lord, consider their threats and enable your servants to speak your word with great boldness. Stretch out your hand to heal and perform signs and wonders through the name of your holy servant Jesus.' After they prayed, the place where they were meeting was shaken. And they were all filled with the Holy Spirit and spoke the word of God boldly."

None of our heroes were above admitting their need of grace to overcome their fears.

And it's scary for a reason . . . because that's when we turn to God and admit our need for help. And guess what? That's when the power rushes in.

At the heart of our hesitation lurks our unspoken fears. But being nervous or afraid doesn't need to stop you anymore than it did Paul and the twelve apostles. The way of power doesn't avoid fear—it passes through it, because fear teaches us to lean on him.

While we're talking about fear, here are the three main fears that freeze fledgling disciple-makers:

- Fear of the unknown
- Fear of inadequacy
- Fear of rejection
- **Fear of the unknown?** *Just show up.* God never asked you to approve any plans, just to take the next step. You walk by faith, not by forecast. Would Bilbo have gone if he knew what awaited him at the start? Probably not. But would he have traded it after the journey ended? Not for the world.
- **Fear of inadequacy?** *You don't feel adequate? Good.* You're in whatever club Abraham, Moses, Gideon, David, Hezekiah, Isaiah, Jeremiah, Peter, and Paul were in. God doesn't call the qualified; he qualifies the called.

* **Fear of rejection?** *Expect it.* Jesus said that if they rejected him, they'll reject us too. I wish I could tell you that doesn't happen. But the best disciple-makers and evangelists on the planet get rejected. Don't take it personally.

Lastly, there's a fear of screwing the whole thing up. But there's no wrong way to make disciples except not to. Still, people will always tell us we're doing it wrong because we do it differently than they do (or, more commonly, don't).

As Dwight Moody once said when someone criticized his approach to preaching the gospel, "It's clear you don't like my way of doing evangelism. You raise some good points. Frankly, I sometimes do not like my way of doing evangelism. But I like my way of doing it better than your way of *not* doing it."[1]

These fears create dependency, or reliance, upon God. But dependency isn't weakness—it's the doorway God's strength walks into your life through. The world says, "Stand on your own two feet." Jesus says, "Remain in me and . . . you will bear much fruit; apart from me you can do nothing" (John 15:5). So if you're feeling weak in the knees, or have a queasy, uneasy feeling in your gut, you're doing it right.

So don't try to prove how strong you are in your disciple-making venture. Instead, embrace your weakness, walking the middle path between debilitating fear and self-reliance. Practice walking between them both in dependence on God. Breathe out all your self-reliance, and breathe in his Spirit—for in your weakness, his power rests on you.

Pray This—

Holy Spirit, I confess my fears of the unknown, inadequacy, and rejection. Left to myself, I either rush out like Samson with my hair cut off or shrink back in fear. But when you are with me, your presence fills me with boldness. When I tremble, remind me that even Paul and the apostles prayed for courage. Give me words when I have none, faith when I feel weak, and love that casts out fear. Keep me in step with you today so that all I say and do points to Jesus. Amen.

---

1. D. L. Moody, quoted in Dave Earley and David Wheeler, *Evangelism Is . . . : How to Share Jesus with Passion and Confidence* (Nashville: B&H Publishing Group, 2010), 16.

Today's Time

* Why do you think the Bible tells so many stories of fearful people: Abraham, Gideon, Moses, David, Hezekiah, and Peter, to name a few?
* Which of the three main fears (of the unknown, inadequacy, and rejection) do you feel most often? How can you depend on the Holy Spirit to overcome that fear?
* Think about a time when you felt unprepared or afraid but stepped out in faith anyway. What did you learn about God's provision and power in that moment?

Today's Tactic: Step into the Unknown

Eleanor Roosevelt is credited as saying, "Do one thing every day that scares you."

Do one small thing today that you've been avoiding because of fear—initiate a conversation, volunteer for a task, or reach out to someone. Afterward, thank the Spirit for being with you in the step.

Big Idea: Fear isn't a sign you're failing; it's a chance to lean harder on the Spirit. His power shows up in your weakness.

Your Lightbulb Moment

DATE ____ / ____ / ____

STEP 26

Disciples Are Sent with Patience

As you enter the home, give it your greeting. If the home is deserving, let your peace rest on it; if it is not, let your peace return to you.

—MATTHEW 10:12–13

The key to this business is personal relationships.

—THE LATE, GREAT, DICKY FOX, JERRY MAGUIRE

Today's Teaching

When Jesus sent them out, he gave them specific instructions to bless every home they came into but to move on if the Lord didn't seem to be working there already. Rather than force things, they were to go with the flow.

Remember Andrew bringing Peter to faith?

After one dinner with Jesus, Andrew couldn't keep it to himself. He didn't fully understand who Jesus was yet, but he knew enough to know his brother *had* to meet him.

"And he brought him to Jesus" (John 1:42).

If you remember from one of the first steps, that's disciple-making in a nutshell. But notice that Andrew didn't say, "Let me explain everything I just heard." He *connected* him to Jesus. He didn't try to rush anything. He simply took that *next step.*

And that takes patience.

God isn't in a hurry. Therefore, disciple-makers aren't either. Paul wrote, "I planted the seed, Apollos watered it, but God has been making it grow. So neither the one who plants nor the one who waters is anything, but only God, who makes things grow" (1 Cor. 3:6–7).

Watching something grow takes patience as well, and Paul likens this kind of word to planting a seed, watering it, and eventually harvesting—but leaving room for the Holy Spirit to perform the miracle of making someone grow. That's why Cru's mantra ends with "leaving the results to God." It takes the burden off you.

If you can introduce people to Jesus, like Andrew did, and leave the results up to God, you'll make plenty of disciples.

The Discipology Plan on the Through the Word app will help you introduce people to Jesus. As they read through John's gospel, God's Word will do most of the heavy lifting, but he will also use your follow-up conversation. Rather than telling them what to think, you'll be listening. It's more important for disciple-makers to be good listeners than good talkers. People who lecture make others want to squirm—that's talking at somebody rather than with them. Patiently listen, knowing that the Holy Spirit is working through his Word.

Jesus was also patient in disciple-making. He didn't walk up to strangers and demand behavior change. He called people by name. He ate with them. He laughed with them. He listened before He led. Before he ever said, "Follow me," he noticed them, saw them, loved them. Disciple-making begins with connection, not correction.

And disciple-making relationships take time. They're inefficient. But they're also the only soil where real discipleship grows.

Oh . . . you also need to be patient with yourself. You're going to be tempted to put it off till you're perfect, but that's a mistake. If you've ever felt disqualified from making disciples because you don't have it all together—good. That means you're exactly the kind of person Jesus can use. Nobody needs your highlight reel. They need your *real life*. The world's had enough of polished Christians who know how to talk the talk but hide their brokenness. What people are hungry for is authenticity. They want to know if this Jesus actually makes a difference when life goes sideways.

So be honest. Let them see your flaws, your questions, your wrestling. Let them know where you've bled. Show them the scars and the grace that healed them. Jesus didn't hide his wounds. They were the proof of his love. Don't be afraid to let others see yours.

Disciple-making isn't about impressing people. It's about showing them what following Jesus *really* looks like—on the good days and the days you're crawling back to grace.

Besides, the goal is not to make someone look like you. It's to help them love Jesus.

When they ask questions, point them to what Jesus said. When they're discouraged, remind them of what he did. When they're stuck in sin, show them how he responded to people just like them. Let the words of Jesus become the ground under their feet. Let the presence of Jesus become the air they breathe. Because in the end, that's what will change them. You're only the guide. *Don't mistake yourself for the destination.*

Be patient with the process. Real discipleship is messy. People are messy. You'll pour into someone, and they'll bail. You'll share your heart, and they won't get it. You'll pray your guts out, and it'll feel like nothing's moving.

Keep loving them anyway, like Jesus did. He discipled twelve men who argued about who was the greatest, fell asleep during prayer, and abandoned him when things got hard. And he still washed their feet. That's the kind of love that disciple-making takes.

Being patient doesn't mean you condone sin but that you understand transformation takes time. Grace works slowly. People who are still learning to hear the Shepherd's voice sometimes wander. Your job is to walk with them, point them back to Jesus, and keep loving them through every detour.

You're not discipling a project. You're walking with a person. So don't quit on them because they're not where you hoped. Neither are you.

You just need to care enough to show up—and to keep showing up. One conversation at a time. One meal at a time. One prayer at a time. Be patient. Don't rush the Holy Spirit. And step out of the way so that God can move and work in your disciple's life.

Pray This

Lord Jesus, you are the one who makes seeds grow. Thank you for letting us take part in your work—whether planting, watering, or reaping. Keep us from thinking it depends on us. Help us to listen well, love deeply, and always point people back to you. Let every conversation, every prayer, every step lead to your presence. Be the center of it all. And allow me the grace to get out of your way and allow you to work. Amen.

Today's Time

* Which areas test your patience?
* Have you ever felt the pressure to do all the "work" yourself to introduce someone to Jesus?
* How can you make sure that Jesus's role in your "who's" life is more important than your role?

Today's Tactic: Listen First

Have a short conversation with someone today where your only goal is to listen. Ask two or three genuine questions and resist the urge to give advice.

Afterward, pray privately that God would use what you heard to lead them closer to Jesus.

Big Idea: Disciple-making takes time. Your role is to sow and water faithfully while God makes things grow.

Your Lightbulb Moment—

DATE ____ / ____ / ____

STEP 27

Disciples Are Sent with Grit

And even the very hairs of your head are all numbered. So don't be afraid; you are worth more than many sparrows.

—MATTHEW 10:30–31

The greatest trick the devil ever pulled off was convincing the world he didn't exist.

—ROGER "VERBAL" KINT, THE USUAL SUSPECTS

Today's Teaching

If you've been following Jesus for any length of time, you've probably noticed something: The moment you step forward in obedience, life gets harder. Disciple-making is no exception. It's like a target is put on your back. And that's not paranoia—it's a promise. Jesus warned his disciples that if they went, they needed to expect a fight. The moment you decide to invest in others, you're stepping onto a battlefield. Disciple-making doesn't happen in neutral territory, but on enemy turf, and the Enemy doesn't take your encroachment lightly. Paul put it plainly: "Our struggle is not against flesh and blood, but against the rulers, against the authorities, against the powers of this dark world and against the spiritual forces of evil in the heavenly realms" (Eph. 6:12). In other words, there's more going on than what you can see.

That means the frustrations and conflicts you face aren't always coincidences. The nagging discouragement that won't leave you. The temptation that pounces when you're tired. The conflict with a coworker or family member that feels bigger than both of you. Sometimes those are flaming arrows meant to distract you, disarm you, or drag you down. And here's why: If Satan can keep you sidelined, the damage is contained. You're only one person. But the moment you start pouring into others, your impact multiplies—and that terrifies the powers of darkness. Every time you open the Word with your two, hell takes notice. Every conversation about Jesus with a who is a threat. Every prayer whispered for someone's salvation, every act of faithfulness advances the kingdom. That's why Satan won't just shrug and walk away. He'd rather hurl discouragement like flaming arrows than risk you reproducing your faith in someone else. Resistance isn't proof you're failing; often it's proof you're right on target.

Jesus knew this, which is why he didn't sugarcoat his words when he sent out the Twelve in Matthew 10. His instructions sounded less like a pep talk and more like a war briefing. He warned them they'd be handed over to councils, flogged in synagogues, dragged before governors. Families would turn against them. They'd be hated because of his name. Not exactly a morale booster, but it was reality. And right in the middle of that, he gave them a promise that steadies us to this day: "Are not two sparrows sold for a penny? Yet not one of them will fall to the ground outside your Father's care. And even the very hairs of your head are all numbered. So don't be afraid; you are worth more than many sparrows" (Matt. 10:29–31).

Read that again. Jesus doesn't downplay the danger. He doesn't pretend arrows won't fly. He looks his disciples in the eyes and says, "You'll take hits, but none of them will land outside the Father's care." Every disciple-maker lives under that same promise: You may feel the sting of arrows, but none can pierce the promise that he is with you.

Paul warned of "flaming arrows" raining from above, meant to intimidate, scatter, and wound (Eph. 6:16). And sometimes they find their mark. You've felt them: the arrow of doubt whispering you're not good enough to disciple anyone. The arrow of discouragement telling you this isn't working. The arrow of distraction nudging you to put off disciple-making until life slows down. The arrow of fear warning you that if you press too far, you'll lose friends, respect, maybe even your job. Those arrows are real. But Paul says "Take up the shield of faith, with which you can extinguish all the flaming arrows of the evil one" (Eph. 6:16). The ancient archers kept the opposing armies at bay—their opponents too afraid to come within range of their arrows. Fear doesn't have to defeat you; it just has to stop you. That's why God gave us the shield of faith so that we can advance without flinching. Churchill has been credited with saying, "Fear is a reaction. Courage is a decision." So decide. Raise your shield and simply take the next step . . . and the next . . .

Having faith means saying, "Even if I feel inadequate, God is able. Even if I don't see fruit yet, he's still working. Even if I'm afraid, he's with me." That's the paradox of disciple-making. On the one hand, you're vulnerable. You'll feel stretched, targeted, under fire. On the other hand, you're invincible. Not because you're tough but because the God who counts sparrows and numbers hairs is covering you. You're not just living sent—you're living shielded.

But although Jesus didn't promise the Twelve safety; he did promise them security—the security of his presence.

Pray This

Father, I didn't ask for a fight, but I won't back down from one either. I know the Enemy is real, and I know he's already been defeated. Fill me with your Spirit. Strengthen me with your truth. And make me dangerous to the darkness. Teach me to fight like Jesus—with truth, trust, and tenacity. I'm not afraid of the valley of shadow, because you are with me in it. Lead me out in power. Amen.

Today's Time

* Where have you experienced spiritual resistance in your life or disciple-making efforts?
* How does knowing God numbers the hairs on your head change how you look at the dangers that come with disciple-making?
* Which particular arrow has the Enemy been reaching for in his quiver in his effort to try to stop you?

Today's Tactic: Battle Plans

Take ten to fifteen minutes to write down a personal "battle plan" for the next time you're under spiritual pressure. Include a list of the following:

* A lie you're prone to believe (e.g., "I'm not enough," "God's holding out on me," "I'm alone in this").
* A truth that counters it. If you know a verse, write it down. If not, try searching the Bible or asking a friend who knows the Word well. It is the shield you'll hold up to extinguish the devil's lies. It's also your sword, which will allow you to fight back with truth.
* A healthy response you can use instead of giving in to fear, shame, or self-sabotage.
* One person you can reach out to when the pressure hits. You're not meant to fight alone.

Big Idea: Making disciples means putting your toe to the line and entering a fight, but Jesus sends his disciples with grit.

Your Lightbulb Moment

STEP 28

Disciples Are Sent with Love

Today's Teaching

Today is the last step in the tactics rhythm. My baby's all grown up! Sorry, I have something in my eye . . .

Like any good story, Jesus's disciple-making journey has an epilogue. By the end of John 20, the resurrected Christ has already conquered sin and death, completed his mission, and appeared to his disciples. The credits should roll. But John gives us one more chapter—his Marvel postcredits scene. And it's all about a single, solitary conversation between Peter and Jesus.

You know Peter's story. He was loud, brash, quick to jump, quick to speak, and on the night Jesus was arrested, quick to deny he even knew Jesus—three times. But then the rooster crowed. Peter locked eyes with Jesus across the courtyard as the soldiers pushed him outside, and the memory branded itself into his soul. Failure has a way of doing that.

So, when we find Peter in John 21, he's back where it all began—in Capernaum, on a boat, fishing. From the shoreline, a familiar voice cuts across the water: "Friends, haven't you any fish?" It's half invitation, half holy trolling. When they answer no, he calls out, "Throw your net on the right side of the boat."

Peter freezes. He's heard that line before. The moment isn't lost on him—Jesus is intentionally rewinding the tape, taking Peter back to his calling. And when the nets fill, Peter can't help himself. He dives headfirst into the water and swims to shore.

On the beach, Jesus is waiting with breakfast. A fire, fish, and bread. But when the meal is finished, Jesus takes Peter aside for a long walk down the beach. Just the two of them. Because Peter doesn't need another miracle right now. He needs to be restored. He needs to know that his failure hasn't disqualified him from the mission.

Three denials, so three questions. "Simon son of John, do you love me?" Peter answers, "Yes, Lord, you know that I love You." Jesus responds, "Feed my lambs." (John 21:15). When Jesus asks the third time, the connection is unmistakable: "Peter was hurt" (John 21:17). But Jesus wasn't trying to wound him; his healing would come through loving the people Jesus loved. People like him. People who got it wrong.

The overlap between loving God and loving people becomes crystal clear. "If you love me, tend my lambs. Care for them. Feed them." Translation? If you love Jesus, disciple his people.

That's the heartbeat of the tactical rhythm. Jesus wasn't handing Peter an abstract idea. He was giving him marching orders for making disciples: Tend the weak. Guide the wandering.

Feed those who get themselves stuck, dirty, and lost—just like the wandering sheep Peter had been. To Jesus, this matters more than anything.

We're tempted to think the "big things" matter most—sermons, stadium crusades, podcasts, platforms. Disciple-making can feel small at times. Sitting with someone over coffee. Explaining Scripture in halting words. Praying with them in whispered faith. When you sit down with your two to read the gospel of John, when you pray for someone who doesn't know Jesus yet, when you invest your time, energy, and affection into another life so they can see Christ, you are loving Jesus.

"If you love me, feed my sheep."

Jesus equating disciple-making with love means it matters to Jesus. Every act of care is valued, every ounce of patience treasured, every small conversation counts. Jesus wanted Peter to know that loving his sheep was loving him. He wants you to know the same.

The resurrected Christ had forty days on earth before he ascended. Every moment mattered, and yet he chose to spend one of those mornings eating breakfast with his friends and restoring a broken fisherman. That tells you everything you need to know about his priorities. He was still disciple-making. Shepherding others was not a side project to Jesus. If it was worth Jesus appearing on a beach, to restore Peter, it would be worth the rest of Peter's life to love Jesus back by doing the same for others. Now Peter knew: Discipling others was central to what it meant to love Jesus.

I don't know what your failures look like. Maybe you've denied Jesus by your silence. Maybe you've stumbled in sin and part of you wonders if he can really use you. Hear this: Failure is never final. Not when Jesus is willing to take a long walk down the beach with you and tell you that loving him means loving failures just like you.

So as you step out onto your disciple-making journey from here, remember that long walk down the beach. Remember a broken fisherman restored. Remember the risen Savior who cooks us breakfast to spend time with us. And remember him saying, "What you do for others is taken as love for me." Every disciple-maker walks that same shoreline. And every time you choose to invest in another person, you're answering the same question: "_____, do you love me?"

"Yes, Lord. You know I love you."

"Feed my sheep."

This is the adventure. This is the call. And Jesus says it's how you love him.

Pray This

Jesus, thank you for not giving up on me when I fail. Thank you for meeting me in my weakness and restoring me with your love. I hear your call today—"Do you love me? Feed my sheep."—and I want to answer yes. Teach me to love you by caring for the people you've placed in my life. Help me to see disciple-making not as a task but as a way of showing you my love. Give me patience with the wandering, tenderness with the weak, and courage with the difficult. Let me never forget that what I do for others I do for you. And may my life echo Peter's lesson—that loving you means loving your people.

Today's Time

* Jesus didn't just ask Peter *if* he loved him; he tied love to action: "Feed my sheep." If Jesus asked you the same question today, what would the evidence of your love look like in the way you care for people?
* Peter's worst failure became the stage for his greatest calling. Where might your own weakness, regret, or shame be the very place Jesus wants to rewrite your story and recommission you?
* Loving Jesus means tending to his people, often in hidden, ordinary ways. Who in your world needs more than a sermon right now—they need a Shepherd? What's one concrete step you can take this week to feed, tend, or protect them?

Scan Me

Today's Tactic: Start John

John's gospel ends with the words of Jesus: "As the Father has sent me, I am sending you" (John 20:21). That wasn't only for Peter and the boys on the beach, it's also for you. The Great Commission is your commission. When you open the gospel of John with your two and your who, you're not just starting another Bible study. You're stepping into the story as a sent one. Jesus is saying, *I'm putting my mission in your hands.*

- If you haven't yet, start the gospel of John with your who on the Through the Word app.
- Celebrate the completion of your Jedi training! Woot! Look out, Empire of evil! Here come the rebels!

Big Idea: We're sent in the same love that sent Jesus—love strong enough to die is strong enough to forgive.

Your Lightbulb Moment —

Conclusion

You made it. Last completion of the Discipology journal—your own journey to disciple-making. But don't start playing "Pomp and Circumstance" just yet, because this isn't graduation—it's the start of your new beginning.

Soon, people will ask if they can invite their friends. Someone will text, "Hey, can my buddy come with me?"

So what do you do? Option A: Tell them this is a private club for Satan's helpers (forgive the *Pee-wee's Big Adventure* reference). Please don't pick A. Option B: Tell them you'll start another group just for them. Solid answer. Option C: Let them jump right in with you. Also a solid answer. Which one's right? That depends on your context, your bandwidth, and most importantly, what the Spirit is prompting. The point is: Don't slam the door. Remember, the first disciples brought their friends along without hesitation until there were six. It may not just be you, your two, and your who. You may have a new small group on your hands.

At a certain point, you'll need to make some decisions. Do you bring them back to your small group, or do you just keep going as you are? It's probably best to talk that over with your leaders, but one thing is certain—if you're making disciples like Jesus did, they'll eventually be going through the same process you just did in these fifty-two steps. And when you have finished discipling them, they will eventually be sending out disciples themselves. And that is exactly what Jesus set into motion two thousand years ago—and how his kingdom still spreads today—through everyday disciple-makers just like you!

A JOURNEY THROUGH JOHN

This next section is your space *to walk with your who* through the gospel of John. Over twenty-four steps, you'll journey alongside John's 21 chapters. Here, you'll record the real stuff: the struggles your who is facing, the questions they're wrestling with, their impressions of Jesus, and the fingerprints of God you begin to see in their life. You'll also write down reminders of what to pray for them. Think of it as a living record of disciple-making in motion—your story woven into theirs, both of you learning to follow Jesus more closely in different ways. If you haven't started John's gospel on Through the Word, scan the QR code to get started.

Step 29

John Introduction

___/___/___
DATE

Observations

How It Was

How You Can Pray

Step 30

John 1: Part 1

___/___/___
DATE

Observations

How It Was

How You Can Pray

Step 31

John 1: Part 2

___/___/___
DATE

Observations

How It Was

How You Can Pray

Step 32

John 2

___/___/___
DATE

Observations

How It Was

How You Can Pray

Step 33

John 3

___/___/___
DATE

Observations

How It Was

How You Can Pray

Step 34

John 4

___/___/___
DATE

Observations

How It Was

How You Can Pray

Step 35

John 5

___/___/___
DATE

Observations

How It Was

How You Can Pray

Step 36

John 6

___/___/___
DATE

Observations

How It Was

How You Can Pray

Step 37

John 7: Part 1

___/___/___
DATE

Observations

How It Was

How You Can Pray

Step 38

John 7: Part 2

___/___/___
DATE

Observations

How It Was

How You Can Pray

Step 39

John 8

___/___/___
DATE

Observations

How It Was

How You Can Pray

Step 40

John 9

___/___/___
DATE

Observations

How It Was

How You Can Pray

Step 41

John 10

___/___/___
DATE

Observations

How It Was

How You Can Pray

Step 42

John 11

___/___/___
DATE

Observations

How It Was

How You Can Pray

Step 43

John 12

___/___/___
DATE

Observations

How It Was

How You Can Pray

Step 44

John 13

___/___/___
DATE

Observations

How It Was

How You Can Pray

Step 45

John 14

___/___/___
DATE

Observations

How It Was

How You Can Pray

Step 46

John 15

___/___/___
DATE

Observations

How It Was

How You Can Pray

Step 47

John 16

___/___/___
DATE

Observations

How It Was

How You Can Pray

Step 48

John 17

___/___/___
DATE

Observations

How It Was

How You Can Pray

Step 49

John 18

___/___/___
DATE

Observations

How It Was

How You Can Pray

Step 50

John 19

___/___/___
DATE

Observations

How It Was

How You Can Pray

Step 51

John 20

___/___/___
DATE

Observations

How It Was

How You Can Pray

Step 52

John 21

___/___/___
DATE

Observations

How It Was

How You Can Pray

APPENDIX

How to Use This Book

Hey, nerds! You took the bait and came to the engineering part of this book. This is where we rip the back panel off the television and let you pull all the insides out to see how it works. Shall we start?

Every journey involves walking, and every walk has multiple steps. The goal of this journey is to learn to walk in the same rhythms of disciple-making that Jesus did. Those three rhythms were time, teaching, and tactics. So this journal includes those three rhythms in every step.

Every step you take will include the following:

Teaching: Each teaching contains a disciple-making story and the principles for you to put into practice. In addition to the written teaching in this journal, there's also a Discipology Plan audio guide on the Through the Word app to listen to when you're on the go. The teaching on the ten-minute audio guide and the written part in your journal cover the same step but are not the same exact content. The written teaching in this journal is a reference for you to read and come back to whenever you need it. Listen or read, or do both!

Time: Each step also allows for time to reflect with your disciple-making partner. The journal lets you write privately, and the Discipology Plan on the Through the Word app lets you share and discuss with your disciple-making partner.

Tactics: Each day we give you one simple action step. Nothing monumental—just the next step right in front of you. Remember, Rome wasn't discipled in a day.

Lastly, at each step on this journey, you will have a lightbulb moment. It is your biggest takeaway from that step: what the Holy Spirit was saying to you most powerfully—your personal aha or eureka moment. And here's the cool part: It doesn't always come from the same rhythm (time, teaching, or tactics). Each day will be different, but the important thing is that you capture that lightning in a bottle. You will always be able to look back on these as your own personal journey of discovery.

For every long journey bringing the right gear is a game changer. Everything you'll need is found in this journal and the Discipology Plan on the Through the Word app. The app is simple to use and totally free—with no ads or hidden costs. You'll also be using it later to invite your friends on the journey. So go ahead, scan the QR code below, and let the app walk you into the Discipology Plan.

The Road Ahead

There are fifty-two steps in this journey. But don't worry, you won't have to figure out the journey on your own. I'll walk you through it, one small step at a time. We'll put trail markers along the journey so that you can know where you're walking.

Think of it like a long walk—you don't get to the end in a single stride. You just keep putting one foot in front of the other, and before you know it, you've covered miles you never thought you could. Each day's step might feel small, but they all add up to a lifetime of following Jesus and helping others do the same.

You can break up this journey in one of two ways:

A daily journey: Taking one step per day, you can use this journal like a devotional and be finished in fifty-two days—just under two months!

A weekly journey: Since there are 52 weeks in a year, you can also break it up into a year-long journey, taking one step every week.

Whatever timeline works best for your journey, for the first half, you'll be training; for the second half, you'll be doing.

First Half of the Disciple-Making Journey

Activity: Training
Focus: Discipology Plan
Steps: 28
Who: You and your two

Jesus always sent his disciples out in pairs. You don't have to go this alone, and having someone with you relieves some of the burden and makes it less intimidating. Throughout this journal we will refer to your disciple-making partner as your "two." So your first assignment will be to grab your two, who will train alongside you. Be sure to recruit them before starting the journey, and encourage them to get a journal as well.

Second Half of the Disciple-Making Journey

Activity: Doing
Focus: Gospel of John Plan
Steps: 24
Who: You, your two, and a who

You and your two will start to disciple a "who." Your who is the person you'll help follow Jesus. Together, you and your two will walk alongside the who—the three of you together will walk alongside Jesus and the disciples through the gospel of John. There are twenty-four gospel of John audio guides on the Through The Word app. Just like you processed what you were learning with your two during the first half, so the three of you will interact with John's gospel and help the who wrestle with who Jesus is. This is real disciple-making, and I can't wait for you to go on this journey. It will be incredible!

Using This Journal with a Small Group

There is another way to use this book. Although you and your two can do this independently, it was designed to be used within a church context as well, especially to complement the work of a small group.

Your whole small group or youth group can pair off and step into making disciples together, whether for a two-month stretch or weekly over the course of a year. In either of those timelines, you and your two gather with your small group, youth group, or any other type of group (singles, career, men's or women's groups), and scatter during the week to make disciples.

Disciple-making with a small group is like breathing—you inhale and exhale. Gather and scatter. Which is more important, inhaling or exhaling? Try skipping one, and you'll quickly find out: One fuels the other. Gathering gives you encouragement, scattering gives you opportunity.

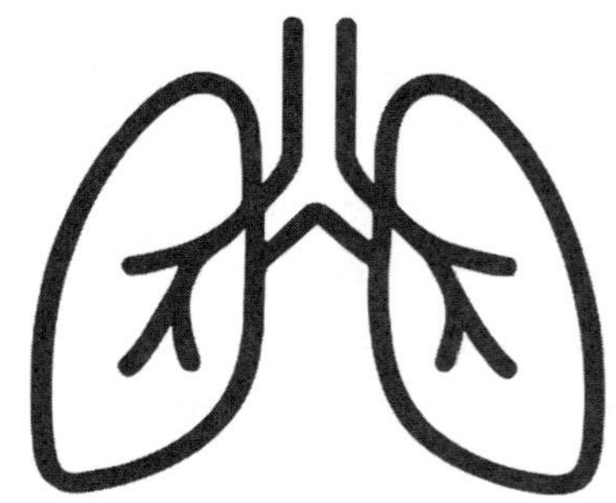

When you gather with your small group, it's like taking a deep breath in—praying, sharing stories, encouraging each other, and getting reenergized. And when you scatter, it's the breath going out—seeing the Spirit move through you in real life. Scattering just makes you eager to get back to gathering to celebrate wins and share stories of God at work.

That's why we have designed a small group study to accompany this journal for those of you who would like to have a guide for the times when you gather. Again, you can find this and other free resources to accompany your journey at journey.discipology.com.

Well, that's it. I can't wait for you to get started!

In summary, this journal is your road map. The app is your guide. Your two is your travel companion. And your who? They're the reason you set out on this road in the first place.

Journey Farther.

If you're ready to take your disciple-making off-road, you'll find everything you need to keep moving: tools that sharpen your skills and training that multiplies disciple-makers.

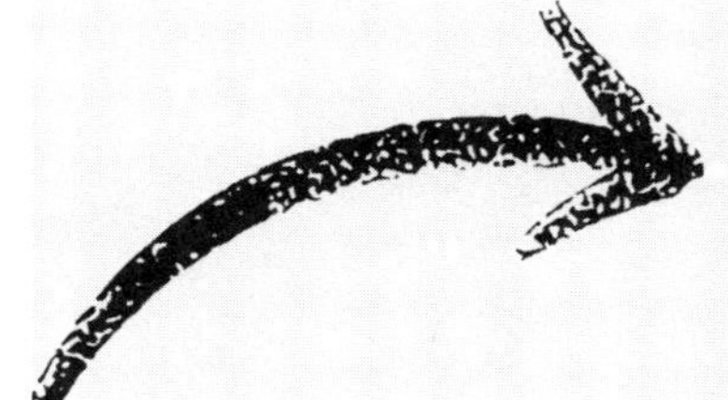

Explore what's next at journey.discipology.com